A Woman's Guide to Success:

Perfecting Your Professional Image

Doris Pooser

THOMSON

COURSE TECHNOLOGY

Professional ■ Trade ■ Reference

Publisher and General Manager of Course PTR: Stacy L. Hiquet

Associate Director of Marketing: Sarah O'Donnell

Marketing Manager: Kristin Eisenzopf

Manager of Editorial Services: Heather Talbot

PTR Editorial Services Coordinator: Elizabeth Furbish

Acquisitions Editor: Mitzi Koontz

Editor: Jenny Au

Project Editor: Sandy Doell

Market Coordinator: Jordan Casey

Interior Layout Tech: William Hartman

Cover Designer: Mike Tanamachi

Indexer: Katherine Stimson

Always in Style® is a registered trademark of AIS Marketing Services, Inc.

All other trademarks are the property of their respective owners.

Important: Course PTR cannot provide software support. Please contact the appropriate software manufacturer's technical support line or Web site for assistance.

Course PTR and the author have attempted throughout this book to distinguish proprietary trademarks from descriptive terms by following the capitalization style used by the manufacturer.

Information contained in this book has been obtained by Course PTR from sources believed to be reliable. However, because of the possibility of human or mechanical error by our sources, Course PTR, or others, the Publisher does not guarantee the accuracy, adequacy, or completeness of any information and is not responsible for any errors or omissions or the results obtained from use of such information. Readers should be particularly aware of the fact that the Internet is an ever-changing entity. Some facts may have changed since this book went to press.

Educational facilities, companies, and organizations interested in multiple copies or licensing of this book should contact the publisher for quantity discount information. Training manuals, CD-ROMs, and portions of this book are also available individually or can be tailored for specific needs.

ISBN: 1-59200-924-7

Library of Congress Catalog Card Number: 2005923960

Printed in the United States of America

05 06 07 08 09 BU 10 9 8 7 6 5 4 3 2 1

THOMSON

COURSE TECHNOLOGY™

Professional ■ Trade ■ Reference

Thomson Course Technology PTR, a division of Thomson Course Technology
25 Thomson Place ■ Boston, MA 02210 ■ http://www.courseptr.com

To my Granddaughter
Karina Pooser

Acknowledgments

With the interest in Western dress and style for both corporate men and women in China over the last several years, I was delighted to be offered a contract for publication of my books, *Always in Style* and *Successful Style for Men*. However, the publisher also wanted a corporate book for women. I suggested that I revise, update, and expand the original *Successful Style for Men* book and do a version for women. *Always in Style, Secrets of Success for Women,* and *Secrets of Success for Men* will all be published in April 2005 in China.

Since I have never done a woman's career book that includes wardrobe planning, body language, business, and dining etiquette in the United States and there is still confusion about casual business and career dressing, proper business etiquette, especially between men and women colleagues, and more interest than ever in personal style as witnessed by the popularity of the extreme makeover shows, I thought that perhaps the timing was right for a book that women could use as a reference for developing a successful personal style.

I am grateful that Thomson Course Technology PTR agreed and has published *A Woman's Guide to Success: Perfecting Your Professional Image.*

Some of the topics covered in *A Woman's Guide to Success: Perfecting Your Professional Image* have been covered in more

A Woman's Guide to Success:
Perfecting Your Professional Image

detail in my *Always in Style* and *The Essential Guide to Hair, Make-up, and Skin Care* books. However, I have included a summary and the latest updates on some of these topics including color, bodyline, and make-up and have presented a simple guide for getting ahead in your personal and professional life.

Always in Style was first published over twenty years ago, is in its seventh printing, and is still selling. Thanks to the many women and men who have taken my training and have subscribed to the Always in Style® membership program on www.alwaysinstyle.com, I have been able to update, fine-tune, and further confirm the accuracy and success of the Always in Style® concepts.

As always, many people have contributed to making this book a possibility. I am so very grateful for their support, input, and commitment to Always in Style and to me personally. Special thanks to Jenny Au for her incredible talent and dedication to Always in Style in the U.S. and in China; to Carole D'arconte for helping me stay on top of the trends and providing many of the images contained in the book; to Robert Hickey for his continued support and etiquette expertise; to the Always in Style team: Reenie Henry, Margaret O'Malley, Thayooru Nandanraj, and Sumita Ohri.

Acknowledgments

A special thanks to my wonderful family and friends for always being there for me: to my son Jeff and his family Amy and Karina Pooser, to my son Todd Pooser and Kim Palumbo, to my sister and niece, Joan and Molly Molvik, to Carole Tucker, Pam Abeling, and Marj Adler for never wavering in their friendship over all the years.

And to all those at Thomson Course Technology: Mitzi Koontz, Sandy Doell, Bill Hartman, Kristin Eisenzopf, and Katherine Stimson—I appreciate all of your help and input.

A Woman's Guide to Success:
Perfecting Your Professional Image

Doris Pooser, a recognized expert in the fashion and beauty industry for over 25 years, has helped thousands of women and men to look and feel their best. Doris is the author of several best selling books on personal style for both men and women, and is editor of the *Always in Style Seasonal Trend Report,* which brings the best looks from the runway collections to everyday women and men.

Doris has reached millions as a style expert through her speaking engagements, television broadcast appearances on all of the major networks as well as Lifetime, CNN, and Fox, and on her own shows on QVC. She has attracted media attention from some of the most respected names in women's publishing, including *Marie Claire, Woman's World, O Magazine,* and Oprah.com.

Doris' speaking career has included keynote addresses for major corporations interested in image, presentations skills, etiquette, and personal packaging. Doris says, "Looking good creates not only a positive first impression but

improves self image, self esteem, and confidence, all necessary to achieve success in business and in our personal lives."

In addition to her individual reach, Doris has also trained thousands of image consultants, personal shoppers, and sales associates in over 17 countries using the techniques she developed in her Always in Style® program. Sales staffs in notable department stores such as Nordstrom, Bloomingdales, and JC Penney have been trained using the Always In Style® program.

Using the Always in Style® concepts and extensive databases she developed over the years, Doris has created a proprietary Personal Profile® software program for use as a personal shopping tool that provides advice and recommendations for consumers based on their individual needs and physical characteristics.

Whether it is in a group or an individual situation, Doris' workshops, lectures, books, fashion trend reports, and Web site strive to create personalized and targeted style and

A Woman's Guide to Success:
Perfecting Your Professional Image

fashion advice and inspiration for every woman or man. For more information about Doris, please contact her at doris@alwaysinstyle.com.

Speaking Topics

In an entertaining and informative program, Doris has over 25 years of experience addressing these important topics:

- Image & Personal Style Presentation Skills, Personal Packaging & Body Language
- Travel & Dining Etiquette
- Men & Women: Relationships in the Workplace, Wardrobe Essentials & Self Esteem
- Presentations will be focused and targeted to the needs of the client and may include some of the following titles:

  * Successful Style
  * The Secrets to Success
  * Getting Ahead in Business and Your Personal Life
  * Gaining the Competitive Edge
  * Building Self Confidence
  * Looking Good and Feeling Good
  * The Woman Entrepreneur/ Women in Business

Books

Always in Style With Color Me Beautiful: Your Shape, Your Style! (Acropolis Books, Inc.; 1985)

Always in Style: Develop your own personal image with shape and colour (Piatkus; 1987)

Successful Style: A Man's Guide to a Complete Professional Image (Crisp Publications; 1989)

Secrets of Style: Your Personal Profile: Style, Bodyline, Wardrobe, Color, Hair, Make-Up (Crisp Publications; 1992)

Always in Style: The Revised Edition of the Acclaimed Classic on Creating Your Personal Style: Style, Bodyline, Wardrobe, Color, Hair, Make-Up (Crisp Publications; 1997)

The Essential Guide to Hair, Make-up & Skin Care: Always in Style (Crisp Publications; 2000)

Doris' books have sold over 500,000 copies and have been published in seven countries.

A Woman's Guide to Success:
Perfecting Your Professional Image

Jenny Au

Always in Style Vice President (China) Contributor, Co-Editor, Artist, Doris Pooser's *Secrets of Success: Your Personal Style*

"Doris has a natural way of making us feel confident in our style and beauty."

For more information about Jenny, please contact her at jenny@alwaysinstyle.com.

Contents

A Woman's Guide to Success: Perfecting Your Professional Image

Introduction

TO: PROFESSIONALS ON THE WAY TO THE TOP

Successful style is for women who know that style counts!

Style really does, whether in your career or in your personal life. Look at a woman you admire. Have you noticed that she looks self confident, well-dressed, and successful whether she is at the gym, at work, or at a party? She projects a positive first impression, and you can say with certainty that she has a personal style.

Attend a board meeting anywhere in the world. Those seated around the table may be different when it comes to ideas, ambition, drive, or their tastes. But they all project a positive image and have the desire to look the best they can, which is one of the reasons they are where they are—at the top.

Over the years, I have worked with many men and women throughout the world from all walks of life. Many are at the top of their professions—and still I have found that they have a need to know and are interested in fine-tuning their personal image and style. They understand the importance of a positive first impression and the impact it has in their professional and personal lives. And for those who are just beginning their careers or looking for a way to achieve their dreams, it has been shown over and over again that first impressions do matter.

A Woman's Guide to Success:
Perfecting Your Professional Image

I recently held a seminar for a group of independent business women in the beauty industry. My mission was to define style and relate it to the women, individually. It produced some eye opening results.

I asked a group to come on stage to help in the experiment. Just by looking at them, I told them, I could choose the most successful—the one I would trust with giving me advice and from whom I would buy.

Six volunteered. I watched the women as each came on stage. I noticed their clothing, hair, make-up, posture, and walk. I picked the last woman in the group, the one I would trust with my business. I picked the most successful woman.

I had no advance knowledge, yet she projected confidence, taste, power, and ease. Notice that this was not just about how she dressed, but about her total presentation.

One of the others was a bit surprised and asked, "What's so different about the way I look compared to her?"

So as to be positive, I pointed out what I noticed within the first 30 seconds about the winner. Her clothing fit properly. The colors that she wore complemented her. Her make-up was applied so that it looked natural and professional. Her hair complemented her face shape. Her skirt and jacket were the current fashionable

Introduction

lengths. Her shoes and hose were coordinated and stylish. Her posture was straight, and she was poised and confident throughout the experiment.

This isn't to suggest that appearance is everything. But one thing is certain: if you look as if you belong at the top and feel successful, you have taken the first step in getting there.

Obviously, ideas about style, taste, and grooming have a way of becoming blurred by opinions. In the 70s, we experienced the "hippie" movement, where women wore no make-up, poorly fit clothing, and looked less than well groomed. In the 1990s during the dot.com explosion, there was a deliberate attempt to look "unsuccessful," and send out an anti-establishment message. Many of the young entrepreneurs prided themselves on their lack of style and wore things that might not be considered appropriate by some for the back porch.

Their new age ideas of how to run businesses and how to dress soon proved unsuccessful to many. Thousands of dot.com companies went out of business by the end of 2000. Those that did succeed may still favor "casual wear" for work, but those at the top from Michael Dell to Steve Case to Bill Gates, Andrea Jung, Carly Fiorina, all dress with style, their own unique style, with taste and appropriateness.

A Woman's Guide to Success: Perfecting Your Professional Image

My focus in this book is on "total presentation," the mix of verbal and non-verbal signals. It has been proven that people who make positive impressions non-verbally (looking great) and who follow up with strong verbal presentation are more confident, get the best opportunities, and will be more successful in achieving their goals in life.

A Woman's Guide to Success: Perfecting Your Professional Image comes to you with a promise: to help you develop your style and total presentation in an easy, simple, and step-by-step way. If you are going to look good, feel good about yourself, and achieve success, this book is your answer.

> It has been shown that within the first
> 30 seconds that you meet someone they form an
> opinion about you.
>
> 55% is how you look
> 38% is your presentation: voice and body language
> 7% is what you have to say.
>
> *A Woman's Guide to Success: Perfecting Your
> Professional Image* can get you 93% of the way to
> making a positive first impression and unlocking
> the door to personal success.

Part 1

Rules of the Road

In this section of *A Woman's Guide to Success: Perfecting Your Professional Image,* you will learn the ABCs of what it takes to make the most of your appearance and how to craft your own special style.

The basics, outlined in Chapter One, will provide you with a wardrobe plan for formal business, casual business, leisure, and important formal occasions.

You will also learn how to personalize your wardrobe so that it heightens your strong points and minimizes weaknesses.

I want to emphasize that the skills are based on solid, time-tested methods; they are not a collection of vague opinions, fads, or fancies. There is a definite science behind the "art" of personal appearance, and this, as much as possible, will be your guide.

Keep in mind that the principles of personal style are much less subjective than you might have imagined. Those discussed here have worked for thousands of men and women worldwide; they are empirical and can be tested. After all, if your appearance is critical to succeed in your professional and personal life, it is far too important to be left to feelings of iffy concepts of taste. Making it to the top isn't a guessing game. Learning taste and style or fine tuning it is possible.

Style starts with being well-dressed. Throughout this book we will be working with the following definition of being WELL-DRESSED.

The well-dressed woman wears clothes, accessories, hairstyles, and make-up that:

- Complement her physically
- Express her personality
- Are appropriate for the occasion and
- Are current and fashionable

Being well-dressed is the first step in projecting confidence and a sense of style.

I believe you will find these simple rules to be exciting and rewarding. Being the best you can be is an adventure of self-discovery, and that is really the goal—to discover those personal qualities that lend to self confidence, satisfaction, and the highest rewards.

1 Wardrobe Basics

YOUR BASIC PLAN

Formal Business

Casual Business

Leisure Wear

The Extras

To succeed at anything worthwhile you need a basic plan, a plan that is right for you and is custom-made for your needs.

Companies have their own dress codes, which may or may not be clear to their employees, never mind their customers and affiliates, often resulting in less than consistent messages. No company would consider not standardizing and having professionally designed stationery, business cards, and corporate materials. And yet their employees or representatives may not have been given clear guidelines in how to dress and present themselves. It is up to you to ask for clarity and then take it upon yourself to make the most professional presentation, using the guidelines below. You will be starting with a big advantage.

Remember also that each company has its own well (or not so well) described dress code. It is always acceptable, and in fact preferable, to call ahead of your meeting and ask what the dress code for that particular company or day is, and dress accordingly. If this is not possible, play it safe. It is better to be "over dressed," from a professional point of view, than under dressed.

In this chapter we will outline three basic wardrobe plans, essentially the minimum you will need for formal business, casual

A Woman's Guide to Success: Perfecting Your Professional Image

business and leisure wear, and the extras you can use to make the most of formal occasions.

The plans are based on surveys of hundreds of executives and professionals operating in a wide spectrum of business environments from entrepreneurial start-ups to "mega-corps" such as General Electric, General Motors, Microsoft, Disney, and Revlon. The executives surveyed were asked to list their basic wardrobe pieces, including number of suits, dresses, skirts and tops, shoes, and other items they deemed absolutely essential to their activities at work and during their off hours. We averaged the numbers and made adjustments for our objective, a bare bones basic wardrobe plan, and came up with the following.

WARDROBE PLANS

Years ago it was the men who had it easy. They could wear a suit to any business meeting and be appropriately dressed. Today it has become more of a challenge for men than for women to determine what to wear to that meeting. What exactly does "casual" or "business" dress mean?

In the past, women had to decide whether to wear a dress, slacks, a skirt, what kind, what fabric, etc. The dress codes today and women's fashions make it easy. A three-piece suit, wool, silk, or a blend with a simple jacket, skirt, and slacks can take you from the business meeting to the most formal cocktail party to the most

"When you shop, always buy the best that you can afford."

"Fit is everything."

1 Wardrobe Basics

casual sporting event anywhere in the world. Slacks are interchangeable with skirts for all occasions, unless your company has a strict rule and requires skirts. Without a mandate, it is a matter of personal choice. With a casual tee shirt, lace teddy, or silk blouse, and a change of accessories, you can go from work to play to evening and be appropriately dressed. A simple black dress can be paired with a jacket and pumps for work, worn with flats for casual, and dressed up with strappy heels and great jewelry. With the items below you will always have "the right thing to wear."

For more formal business meetings, wear a matched suit: skirt and jacket, or slacks and jacket. For less formal, mix and match pieces as separates, the tweed jacket and solid skirt or black slacks and gray jacket. Wear slacks and more casual tops or combine slacks and skirts with sweater sets and cardigans as jackets for the most casual days.

> *"The best thing is to look natural, but it takes make-up to look natural."*
>
> ~ Calvin Klein

Make-up colors (your make-up wardrobe), quantity and application, and hairstyle choices are equally important for consistency in your corporate style. Choosing the right colors and styles will be discussed later.

In planning the basic corporate wardrobe, start with two neutral colors and one or two accent colors to build a capsule wardrobe.

Neutral colors are the foundation for the basic investment pieces.

Neutrals are no-color colors such as gray, black, navy, tan, taupe. Investment pieces are your jackets, skirts, and more formal slacks. Example: (color choices for your unique coloring will be discussed later.)

- One black suit
- One black and white check or tweed suit or jacket and skirt, to mix and match with black suit
- Red, yellow, black, and white blouses, sweaters, and tops
- Scarves combining these colors

Next add a taupe or gray suit to mix and match with black suit, turquoise, coral-pink, and black blouses, sweaters, and tops. The red and yellow from above also work with this group and vice versa; add scarves combining these colors.

BASIC CORPORATE WARDROBE

Suits

If possible buy a three-piece suit: jacket, skirt, and slacks all matching, for most versatility. If the jacket comes with a skirt or pants only, buy the third piece at the same time to coordinate. These should be in a classic style, matching buttons, no contrasting trim, in a quality wool, silk, cotton, or blend. A blazer and coordinated skirt and pants can be substituted for one suit. Start with a single suit and add to it. Listed are the recommended

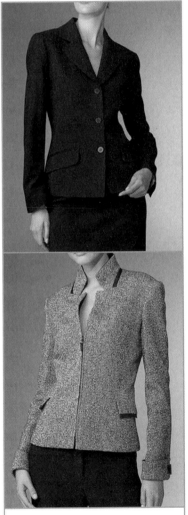

Seamed Suit by Tahari
Tweed Jacket & Pants by Albert Nipon

1 Wardrobe Basics

Tweed Suit by Tahari
Tweed Suit by Laundry by Shelli
Segal

colors from the most formal and serious business colors to the more fashion related shades and patterns.

- One solid (black, gray, or navy) These are the most serious business neutrals
- One solid in color that can be mixed with the first suit (taupe, tan, aubergine, burgundy) or
- One pattern: pin stripe, check, tweed, herringbone (in colors that can mix with the solid above)
- Next add a suit in a great new fashion color and one that complements your coloring

Skirts and Slacks

- Start with two pieces either slacks and/or skirts depending on your personal preference and dress code, complementary to the first suit and then add:
- Skirts: Two to three selected in complementary fabrics and colors to work with jackets above. If suit comes with slacks add an extra skirt.
- Slacks: Two to three extra pairs—black or other colors to work with jackets. If suits above come with skirt only, add an additional pair of slacks.

Blouses

- One to two classic white long sleeves
- Two to three solid or print, silk, cotton, blend

Sweaters/Tops

- Five to six basic jewel neckline, V or turtle neck—fine gauge wool, silk, or blend (long and short sleeves)
- Two to three sweater sets or cardigans in solid colors to work with suits

Dresses

- One simple black, knit, silk, rayon, long or short sleeves
- One solid color (one of accent colors), an overall pattern, tweed, or print, classic style, V-neck, jewel-neck, turtleneck

Coats

- One rain coat or trench
- One overcoat—wool, solid, or fine tweed
- One ¾ or short jacket
- Optional (shearling, fur, or faux fur)

Shoes

- Two to three pairs of plain pumps or sling back in neutral, black, brown, tan, or taupe
- Two pairs of flats, ballet, loafer, or oxford
- One pair of good leather or suede dress boots

Turtleneck & Printed Skirt by
Ralph Lauren Black Label
Double-Bow Dress by
Carmen Marc Valvo

1 Wardrobe Basics

Belts

- Two quality leather to match shoes
- One accent color (optional)

Handbags/Briefcase

- Two neutral, tan, black, brown, or mix in good leather—medium size
- One good leather briefcase
- One small dressy bag, envelop, clutch

Accessories

- Three to four silk scarves
- Leather gloves
- Umbrella
- Watch, leather band or metal—non digital
- Basic earrings: gold, silver, pearls, small to medium size
- Necklace: gold chain, pendant, or pearls
- Brooch or decorative pin
- Simple gold or silver bracelet

> *"Deciding what to wear beyond the dress is not easy, but it makes the difference between elegance and non-elegance. The wrong accessories are the most common mistakes women make."*
>
> ~ Giorgio Armani

EXTRAS FOR CASUAL ACTIVITIES

They are not advisable for corporate dress. More or less of these items can be added based on personal needs. These casual extras can be combined with the more formal pieces above for a casual but stylish look for that day off from work. Combine that great suit jacket with a tee shirt and jeans. Or wear that tweed jacket over a cocktail dress for evening.

Bottoms

- Three to four pairs of jeans, cargos, drawstring, leggings, khakis
- Three to four pairs of shorts, cropped pants
- Two to three pairs of denim, suede, western, novelty

Tops

- Six to eight cotton tee shirts, polos or henleys, cotton sweaters, both long and short sleeve

Shoes

- Sneakers
- Running shoes
- Casual boots
- Sandals
- Flats

Jean Jacket & Pants by Go Silk
Jersey Hoodie & Cargo Mini by
M Missoni

1 Wardrobe Basics

Sports and Exercise

Add appropriate attire for golf, tennis, jogging, hiking, bicycling, exercise, skating, whatever your favorite activity. Many of the pieces in today's active wear collections can double for leisure wear. Leggings, parkas, knit tees, golf shirts, and shorts provide multiple uses while still presenting stylish options at "play."

> *"Dressing is a way of life."*
>
> ~ Yves Saint Laurent

Quilted Jacket & Silk Jeans by Go Silk

Velour Tracksuit by St. John Sport

A Woman's Guide to Success:
Perfecting Your Professional Image

Formal Wear

Depending on the number of formal affairs that you attend, this list will vary. Separates provide maximum versatility and varied combinations.

- One dressy skirt in a fashionable length for the season
- One pair of dressy slacks
- One lace blouse or top
- One satin, silk, sheer, or decorated blouse or top
- One dressy tank, camisole, or bandeaux
- One dressy jacket, sweater, or stole, to be used as an outer piece
- One pair of dressy sandals, silk or metallic pumps, or sling backs
- Small evening bag
- Jewelry—diamond, rhinestone, crystal, or gemstones
- Long shawl in velvet, silk, fur, or faux fur

Black Dress with Belt by Abs by Allen Schwartz
Trompe L'oeil Dress by Dolce & Gabbana

1 Wardrobe Basics

The following list and recommended plan will provide an insight for you when creating a shopping list of "must haves." They will update and coordinate all the pieces already in your closet as well as serve as a guide for starting new capsule wardrobes.

For those who are starting from scratch, it is important to start with a plan, stick with it, and buy the best quality you can afford for your basics.

> *"I believe that style is the only real luxury that is really desirable."*
>
> ~ Giorgio Armani

A Woman's Guide to Success:
Perfecting Your Professional Image

BEGINNERS STARTING BUSINESS WARDROBE

One solid suit
Black, gray, or navy—these are the most serious business neutrals.

One solid suit in color that can be mixed with the first suit (taupe, tan, aubergine, burgundy) or **one pattern:** pin stripe, check, tweed, herringbone (in colors that can mix with the solid above.)

Next add a suit in a great new fashion color and one that complements your coloring.

1 Wardrobe Basics

Skirts and Slacks
Start with two pieces either slacks and/or skirts depending on your personal preference and dress code, complementary to the first suit.

Then add:

Skirts

Two to three selected in complementary fabrics and colors to work with jackets above. If suit comes with slacks add extra skirt.

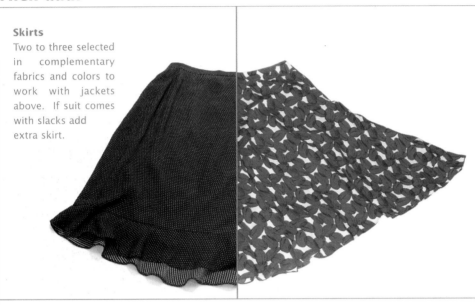

Slacks

Two to three extra pairs (black, and others to work with jackets.) If suits above come with skirt only, add an additional pair of slacks.

1 Wardrobe Basics

Blouses
One white shirt
Two accent colors or prints

Tops/Sweaters
Fine gauge knit, V-neck, turtle neck or jewel neckline

Cardigan or Sweater Set
In solid or pattern to work with slacks and skirts

Dresses

One or two pieces. One simple black, knit, silk , rayon, long or short sleeves. One solid color or overall print (one of accent colors) or print, classic style, V-neck, jewel, turtleneck.

Coats

Rain coat or trench (tan). Overcoat—wool, solid or fine tweed. ¾" or short jacket. Leather, shearling, fur or faux fur (optional)

1 Wardrobe Basics

Shoes

Two to three pairs of plain pumps or sling backs in neutral, black, brown, tan. Two pairs of flats, ballet, loafer, oxford. One pair of good leather or suede dress boots.

Handbags/briefcase

Two neutral, tan, black, brown or mix—medium size. One good leather briefcase. One small dressy bag, envelop, clutch.

Belts

Two good leather to match shoes. One accent color (optional)

Accessories

Three to four silk scarves. Good leather gloves. Umbrella. Watch, leather band or metal—non digital. Basic earring, gold, silver, pearls, small to medium size. Necklace: gold chain, pendant or pearls. Broach or decorative pin. Simple gold or silver bracelet.

PUTTING THE BASIC WARDROBE PLAN INTO ACTION

Now that you have the outline for a basic wardrobe, the next move is learning how to select and personalize each item.

Each of the steps will be discussed in detail later on. For the moment, let's study four primary methods of choosing what is right for you, choosing clothes that complement you physically.

In order of importance, the following steps are essential to making a proper choice:

1. Color: While an item of clothing is still on the rack, select the color that is right for you based on your basic wardrobe plan and your personal color palette. (Part 2 will provide a personalized guide.) In preparing your plan, don't experiment. Consider if you are working on a more formal business wardrobe or one for a more casual work environment or lifestyle. Select neutrals for more formal and serious looks.

> *"Orange is the happiest color."*
>
> Frank Sinatra

"Fashion forward" colors, unusual blends and hues can be fun, but they aren't serious candidates for your "must have" business wardrobe. They can be added later and should be added as you learn to express your personality in your dress style for different occasions. Color may not be everything—but it is important to your personal style. Choose with care.

1 Wardrobe Basics

2. Fabric: We will get into precise selections and recommendations in another chapter, but keep in mind that this category is also important and this selection can be made off the rack. What is critical is that the quality should be the best you can afford, natural fibers and quality blends. In recent years some excellent quality blends and man made fibers are available. For blends, look for at least 55 percent natural fiber.

3. Shape: The item to be chosen has to be taken down from the rack to be studied for proper shaping. However, it can remain on the hanger while you are making up your mind about its appropriateness to you body shape. Later we will discuss body shapes as they related to the cut of various suits and items of clothing. The immediate consideration, however, has to do with the basic silhouette you will get from a particular style you are buying and how it relates to your silhouette.

4. Fit: It has been said that "fit is everything" and there is more than a little truth to this. At this point in the selection process, it is time to try on the item of clothing. Later on you will find a list of things to look for to assure that your clothing not only fits but looks like it was made for you.

Ready to Start

Using the basics here, you will find that you have a basic plan for what items you need, whether you are just starting or are adding to and supplementing your existing wardrobe to make it look the most professional. This all may seem too simplistic, but, in fact, these are the fundamentals. Their proper use is invaluable especially for your career.

Bouclé Multi Zip Jacket, Modal Stretch Crew, and Stretch Sateen Wool Pant by Jones New York

1 Wardrobe Basics

BASIC WARDROBE PLAN CHECKLIST

- Use the lists in Chapter One to outline the articles of clothing you will need for work, during leisure times, and when the occasion demands a more formal look. Make your personal shopping list. Don't deviate even for those great sale items, unless they are things that are on your list. Once you have your basic wardrobe plan completed, you can have fun with extra fashion items on sale. Follow your plan. It will be worth it.

- Go for high quality—the very best you can afford. Remember that the basic pieces of your wardrobe are an investment in your own future. And, like any wise investment, it will pay substantial rewards. For play and casual wear, you can look for less expensive fun items.

- Don't short change yourself. You will need the items recommended. You will want enough to be appropriately dressed for any occasion, a fresh change for each day and a spare for when some items are in the laundry. Better too many than too few when it comes to looking your best.

- The formalizing accessories are critical. To be appropriate for such occasions, you need to dress at least a cut above your best office attire. At some point you may need extras for formal occasions with all of the trimmings, like a formal dress or gown. But in the meantime, the lists provided will give you enough to get by for most affairs. They provide a means of looking "dressy" without overdoing it. Mixing and matching will achieve great results.

- Selecting your clothing in specific order: color, shape, fabric and fit. This is the easiest and most logical way to make your picks. Remember the absolute importance of proper fit, and take your time getting it right. The right color, shape, and fabric can be utterly destroyed by bad fit and tailoring.

2 Basic Looks

WHY DO I NEED ALL THESE CLOTHES?

Lifestyles have changed tremendously in the past 20 years, and both men and women are routinely faced with the demand to adjust their appearance to fit any number of occasions.

Gone are the days when it was enough for men to own a few good suits and a smattering of leisure items and for women to have a basic black dress and a blazer and skirt. Career opportunities have multiplied, and, at the same time, we have been placed in the position of being quick change artists. Today's super mobility requires an office wardrobe, whether casual or more formal, a travel wardrobe, sporting outfits, formal wear, and even special items for the backyard barbeque. Some, especially men, resent these wardrobe demands and steadfastly refuse to give in to the changing patterns of life in this new era; proudly they tell their colleagues how much money they are saving by sticking to a dress code written for a previous generation. That's fine to a point. But these stoic "refusenicks" pay a big price in the long run. Fairly or otherwise, their mobility, socially and professionally, is limited; their appearance says they are either inflexible or unaware (or both!) of the demands of modern life, and the unwritten laws of the times work forcefully against them. Quite frankly their opportunities become frozen.

> *"What do I think about the way most people dress? Most people are not something one thinks about."*
>
> ~ Diana Vreeland

A Woman's Guide to Success:
Perfecting Your Professional Image

Does this mean that you will go as far as the number of outfits hanging in your closet will allow? Well, maybe not. Perhaps you can make it to the top on sheer guts, brains, and force of will. Like the late Howard Hughes, it may be possible to be a millionaire with a single suit, a shirt, one tie, and a pair of well-used sneakers. Maybe. But why, in today's ultra competitive environment would anyone deliberately limit their options? Let's be realistic. If your wardrobe isn't as varied and expansive as the opportunities around you, you are taking more of a risk than you should reasonably be asked to assume. You certainly want diversity in your investment portfolio. And the same prudent, sensible approach needs to be at work with your wardrobe.

LIMITING CLASSIFICATIONS

Between Hollywood, television, fiction writers, lifestyle magazines, and the fashion industry a misconception has arisen that there are different "types of style" that are associated with different "looks."

The natural type: The woman who loves jeans, denim skirts, plaid jackets, boots and uses little or no make-up.

The romantic type: Well-dressed in the latest fashions portraying a very sexy appeal.

The successful type: Dressed in an elegant suit with expensive accessories portraying an air of confidence.

> *"How many cares one loses when one decides not to be something but to be someone."*
>
> ~ Coco Chanel

2 Basic Looks

These images are problematic and confusing, as most clichés tend to be. They are also misleading. The naturalist, the romantic, and the successful executive are one-dimensional cutouts, great if you are dealing in fiction but absurd when it comes to understanding what women are about. In fact, other cutouts can be added to the list, but they would compound the misunderstanding.

Closer to reality is the fact that most people cross all lines, real and imaginary. Real people are as diverse as the situations they find themselves in. Yes, there are "types;" but more often than not they are transformed continually by mood and circumstances. There is only one constant in nature and life: Change!

LOOKS FOR ALL OCCASIONS

In the real world everyone needs different looks for different situations. While they may be more comfortable in certain specific outfits that more-or-less correspond to the clichéd "types," there are times and places that demand different looks.

"Quality ... distinguishes style from fashion."

~ Giorgio Armani

Instead of stereotyping, it is far more practical to define styles of dress that are appropriate for situations that arise constantly in the course of modern living.

Fashion designers have capitalized on this idea, providing endless options with new choices of colors, patterns, and designs each season. Though there is a certain amount of liberation in the choices of style, there is also an overabundance of choices that can be more than slightly bewildering. It is therefore even more important to understand the basics within which to work to select an appropriate and credible wardrobe that fits any occasion.

REAL LIFE LOOKS THAT WORK

Appropriateness for the Occasion

The following looks, or wardrobe designs, correspond to the basic wardrobe plans discussed in Chapter One. Each category describes in a practical way the various looks you'll need to be your best in most situations. The primary logic behind each is "The Big A"—Appropriateness.

Classic Look

Everyone needs a classic look—which translates simply as a conservative look appropriate for business or events such as board meetings, interviews, speaking engagements, political meetings, church. For these occasions, only the classic look is appropriate. Some industries allow for more fashion details but conservatism is the norm.

This classic outfit must physically complement the wearer, it must be of good quality and construction, and importantly, the style must be current.

A Note on Currency Before I Go On

Current doesn't mean "fashion forward" or faddish. A suit of current design is one that isn't obviously outdated. You may recall

3-Piece Wardrober with Empire Belt by George Simonton

2 Basic Looks

the men's suits of the rebellious Flower Power 60s. They had wide lapels (to go with the super wide ties of the era) and trousers were often wide bell bottoms. Wearing such a suit today accompanied with long sideburns, regardless of the quality, says something quite unflattering about that man's sense of style and appropriateness. It says, in the vernacular of the 60s, that you're "out of it!" In the 70s, women headed back to the workplace and were told to dress like men to portray power. Remember the floppy bow ties, teased up bubble hair style, and oxford shoes. Today that is outdated, saying, I'm behind, not aware, or don't care.

Wearing a modern, up-to-date design says you are on top of things, aware of the here and now. That's the critical message of current style and it shouldn't be taken lightly.

Natural Look

Natural can often be interchanged with "casual." For a day off, a picnic, a vacation, or almost any leisure situation, we all need natural looks. The casual work look is not to be confused with the natural look described here. Casual work attire, although not as serious as formal career clothing, which demands a suit or sport jacket and tie for a man and a matched suit for women, still requires a professional look as described by the items in the lists in Chapter One.

Engineered Stripe Jacket with Slim Pants by George Simonton

29

Natural attire for that casual time off can include slacks, jeans, khakis, tee shirts, sweaters, cropped pants, sun dresses. Exercise and athletic wear, and other sports attire are also needed. These items are comfortable, functional, and easy to care for. Included are warm up suits, jogging and tennis outfits, golf clothing, and swimsuits.

Though they represent easy, let-down-and-relax situations, they should be selected for style and quality. Again we come to the matter of appropriateness. There are times and places—the golf course, the country club, a game of squash with a business associate—when you need to consider more than comfort. This isn't license to overdo it with contrived designer outfits, only a caution that the situation requires you to remain aware of the overall image you are hoping to project—your total style.

There is yet another group—"work clothes." There are definitely occasions when covering yourself sans image is fine. When you are working in the garden, painting and doing general chores, utility is the only common sense consideration.

Dressed-Up Look

Here we are dealing with special occasions. Women seem to understand that the special evening out means wearing something special, something more dressy, sexy, or exaggerated. In most cities of the world, evening wear has become more casual.

Angora, Knit Jacket with Faux Crocodile Skirt by George Simonton

2 Basic Looks

For the theatre, fine restaurant, cocktail party, a change in top, some strappy or metallic shoes and dressy earrings and necklace can take you from the office or play to an evening of fun. There are other more formal events, like weddings and dances, when a tuxedo is necessary for men, that elegant ball gowns and cocktail dresses are needed. Men often need to be reminded that the power tie and basic shirt and suit can be dressed up to say this is a special night out. A simple change of the shirt to one with French cuffs or a tone-on-tone and a solid silk tie, says a lot.

High Fashion: Handle with Care

For casual and dressy (non-corporate attire), using the latest, most trendy and high fashion style depends on your personality and lifestyle. Those who are more dramatic, outgoing and like to be different may opt for a more exaggerated look. Those who are more conservative may prefer less trendy styles. There are not just two looks, outdated and high fashion. There are many steps along the way. Reach in a fashion direction according to your personality. But do update, if only with accessories.

Current and Fashionable

"High Fashion" is a loaded phrase. Even in the industry that produces it, there are constant debates about what it actually implies.

Pantchwork Jacket and Pant by George Simonton

A Woman's Guide to Success:
Perfecting Your Professional Image

Despite the controversy, high fashion comes down to a rather simple definition: it is nothing more than an exaggeration of line, scale, color, or detail. Another characteristic is its limited lifetime. Every year (or less) high fashion changes dramatically; if it didn't, it wouldn't live up to its reputation as a fast-paced indicator of the times. Good fashion (less exaggerated) has a 3 to 5 year slowly moving cycle—changes appear slowly and gradually.

High fashion has no place in the traditional corporate environment. I believe this hold true for both sexes. In a business setting "fun clothes" that make a radical statement do just that— they draw attention, they plead for position, and they get in the way. I never recommend exaggeration in developing your own personal style, especially on the job.

However, everyone should be aware of the fashion and the direction it is taking. Think of the fashion direction as a mirror image of what is happening in our society. Museum exhibits, economic conditions, movies, even the political environment influence fashion changes, and we are all aware of this when purchasing

Optic Print Zip Front Jacket by George Simonton

7/8 Wing Collar Jacket & Skirt by George Simonton

2 Basic Looks

refrigerators, cars, computers, homes, boats, sporting gear. New shapes, colors, sizes, and other details continually confront us. They create interest on many levels, and they remind us that life is changing and will continue to change despite our built-in reluctance to accept it. In this sense, "fashion" in clothing is a kind of social barometer, a precursor of things to come.

Though high fashion is inappropriate in most corporate environments, it does enjoy more acceptance in certain fields. Those in the fashion or beauty businesses, advertising, television, public relations, and publishing add high fashion touches all of the time. Since these fields are generally considered "creative" (as opposed to the fiduciary role of a bank official or the expected conservatism of an attorney), those working in these areas can practice moderate amounts of fashion flair. It is acceptable and more-or-less expected of "creative types."

There are also times when everyone can add fashion touches to their appearance. Dressed-up and casual situations offer such flexibility, as do leisure times.

Once again, "You should reach in the fashion direction according to your personality." Have a little fun with fashion.

Cashmere V-Neck Cardigan, Short Sleeve
Jewel Neck Tee, and Windowpane Bouclé
Fluted Hem Skirt by Jones New York

2 Basic Looks

STYLE AND FASHION CHECKLIST

- When it comes to dress, "The Big A"—appropriateness—is as important as what you actually wear. Different occasions demand different looks.

- Avoid "typing" yourself. Your personality is made up of many moods, many strengths. Make your wardrobe fit your diversity.

- Everyone needs a "classic" look, a well made conservative business look, one that complements you physically, is of good quality, and current in style without being trendy.

- Natural and casual clothes are also critical to those on the way up. They should be comfortable and easy to care for. Quality should be high. Even athletic clothing should be right for your overall image.

- When attending a special occasion, dress a cut above your corporate image.

- Think of wardrobe purchases as an investment. When buying, go for quality, classic design, flexibility, durability, comfort, and a flattering fit. They pay big rewards.

- Get rid of outdated clothes. It is important to be in style—not ahead of or behind the curve. Being fashionable doesn't mean "high fashion" or trendy. Current is where you want to be.

- "High Fashion"—an exaggeration in line, detail, or scale. Have fun with these additions to your wardrobe as long as you know exactly when, where, and how to try them out.

- It is important to be aware of fashion trends, just as you are aware of trends in other areas of your life. To avoid them entirely may be playing too safe, and playing too safe conveys a stuffy image.

3 Body Lines

THE SHAPE YOU ARE IN

This chapter is aimed at sizing up your specific body shape and size. Used properly, it is the next best thing to a custom seamstress.

Before you are through, you will understand the styles that suit you best, that flatter you, and make you look the best you can—playing up all of your positive features and minimizing any figure concerns. You will learn how the shape of your face dictates the most complementary hair style, eyeglass frames, collars, jackets, and accessories.

None of this is guesswork or opinion. As promised earlier, the advice offered is based on actual test cases. The formulas I have developed over the years eliminate, as much as possible, the purely subjective variables that sometimes make getting dressed a hit-or-miss proposition. What you will find in the following pages is designed to put your particular body and face into the most flattering and (equally important) comfortable outfits.

"Everything has its beauty, but not everyone sees it"

~ Confucius

A Woman's Guide to Success:
Perfecting Your Professional Image

FASHION IN PERSPECTIVE

Before we go on, a few vital notes on that curious word "fashion" compared with style.

Fashion is a concept that causes a great deal of confusion for many. For some reason, it has taken on a kind of intangible quality; it is mercurial, exclusive, even "elitist," and designers have their own special language. No wonder fashion is viewed as being abstract and indefinable.

WHAT EXACTLY IS FASHION?

Most dictionaries define it as "the way in which something is formed, a configuration." It is also defined as "the prevailing or preferred practice in dress...at a given time." The changes that continue to happen are reflected in changing styles in clothing as well as other consumer products.

Our matching of body and face shapes is based on the first definition; that is, fashion is a "configuration." We put the right shape with the right outfit.

It is the second definition that appears to cause most of the confusion. A preferred manner of dress at a given time leaves the individual facing a 24-hour-a-day infusion of hype and commercial stimuli. It's a matter of custom or choice; it involves juggling the

> *"Fashions fade,
> style is eternal."*
>
> ~ Yves Saint Laurent

3 Body Lines

> *"The goal I seek is to have people refine their style through my clothing without having them become victims of fashion."*
>
> ~ Giorgio Armani

conflicting opinions of everyone around you, not the least of which are the commercial fashion czars who compete for your disposable income and commanding market share.

The end result of this assault on the senses is that many become "fashion victims." Attempting to be stylish, they wind up being trendy or faddish. Their wardrobes become eclectic. And none of this comes cheaply.

THE DIFFERENCE BETWEEN FASHION AND STYLE

Your individual style is you—who you are, your talents, your looks, your personality, your special way of doing things. Your style is forever, and it doesn't change dramatically over the years nor does it change with fashion. It is important to identify your personal style and update it by being aware of the fashion direction.

It is your style that is behind the clothes you select. By defining your body shape as a physically inherent style, it becomes a logical or scientific exercise to pick items that complement this style.

Your clothing has to be personal—a direct and natural extension of you. When you wear clothes that enhance your physical characteristics, it is you and not your clothes that get the most and (the best) attention.

A Woman's Guide to Success:
Perfecting Your Professional Image

For clothes to complement you physically, they need to be right for your body, fit perfectly, and accent your basic coloring. Once you understand your particular characteristics, you will make the right choices. Then it is a matter of keeping up with the changes—fashion—and keeping them in line with your unique style.

If your clothing is to be a natural extension of you, there needs to be a balance, a harmony, between line, scale, and color. The line of your clothing is the silhouette of the outfit and your body. The patterns, fabrics, textures need to harmonize in direct proportion to this line.

The scale—size—should be in proportion to the size of your body. As for color, whatever accent colors you wear should blend and complement your natural skin tone, hair, and eyes.

In the following sections, we will move step-by-step through line, scale, and color. You'll learn how to analyze yourself and determine exactly what to look for when shopping. With this clear cut information in hand, you can overcome bewildering fashion hype and never again become a "fashion victim" or appear outdated.

> *"It pains me physically to see a woman victimized, rendered pathetic, by fashion."*
>
> ~ Yves Saint Laurent

3 Body Lines

THE GEOMETRY OF FACE SHAPES

Before determining your body shape, it is important to accurately determine the shape of your face. The first thing that we see when we look directly at someone is her face. It is part of the total shape a person projects, and therefore the first step in determining your body shape. It allows you to make flattering choices in hair styles, jewelry, clothing, and eyeglass frames. As usual, the idea is to eliminate hit-or-miss perceptions about what is best for you.

Forget ideals. It is really pointless, for instance, to follow the advice of those who insist that hair styles and glasses should somehow change your face shape. It doesn't work that way. After all, your face shape is determined by your DNA. Bone structure and the arrangement of muscle and flesh determine your face shape and body shape. It is certainly possible to correct minor problems, like a narrow or short forehead, a subject to be discussed in a later chapter. But the bottom line is fairly simple: You aren't going to fool Mother Nature. Your face is an immutable part of who you are. Learn to recognize its basic shape and learn to make the best of it.

The standard face shapes are oval, pear, heart, round, rectangle, triangle and square and combinations of these naturally exist. For simplicity we will consider two categories:

Shapes composed of straight lines: Rectangle, square, triangle, diamond as straight shapes.

Shapes made up of curved lines: Round, oval, pear, heart as curved shapes.

Many face shapes are a combination of angles and curves. In determining your face shape we are not looking for an exact label (square or round) but more for an overall shape. Look at the exterior shape as well as your features. Notice if you see more straight lines or angles or more curved lines.

Angled
- Square jaw line
- Defined cheekbones
- Pointed chin
- Straightness on sides
- Angular features
- Straight forehead
- Tapered or slender nose
- Chiseled features
- Almond-shaped eyes
- Straight eye brows

Curved
- Contoured shape
- Round or curved jaw line
- Round or full cheeks
- Round eyes
- Arched eyebrows
- Full lips
- Round or full shaped nose

3 Body Lines

FACE SHAPES

Angled

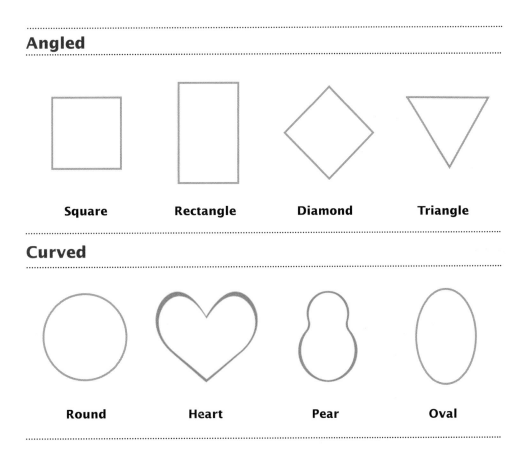

| Square | Rectangle | Diamond | Triangle |

Curved

| Round | Heart | Pear | Oval |

A Woman's Guide to Success:
Perfecting Your Professional Image

FACE SHAPES: ANGLED

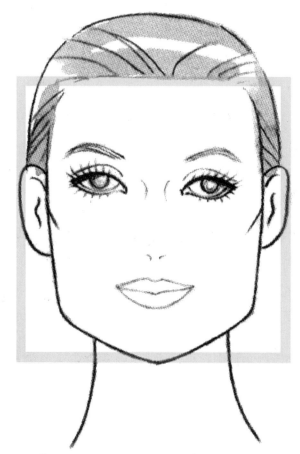

Square
- square jaw-line
- straight sides
- straight hairline at forehead
- flat forehead and/or check area

3 Body Lines

FACE SHAPES: ANGLED

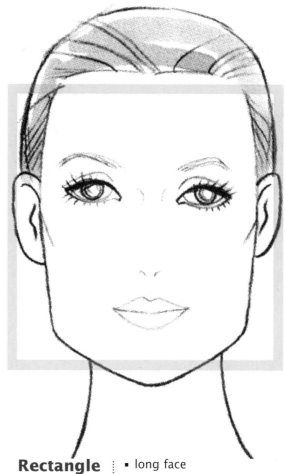

Rectangle
- long face
- square Jaw-line
- square forehead at hairline
- flat forehead and/or check area

A Woman's Guide to Success:
Perfecting Your Professional Image

FACE SHAPES: ANGLED

Diamond
- pointy chin
- prominent cheekbones
- narrow forehead

3 Body Lines

FACE SHAPES: ANGLED

Triangle
- narrow chin
- prominent cheekbones
- broad or wide forehead

A Woman's Guide to Success:
Perfecting Your Professional Image

FACE SHAPES: CURVED

Round
- soft jaw-line
- round cheeks
- curved hairline and forehead

3 Body Lines

FACE SHAPES: CURVED

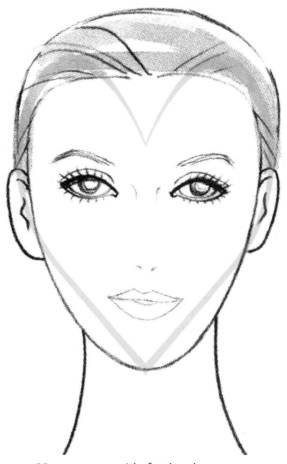

Heart
- wide forehead
- curved hairline or widow's peak
- narrow chin

FACE SHAPES: CURVED

Pear · narrow forehead
· full cheeks
· wide chin

3 Body Lines

FACE SHAPES: CURVED

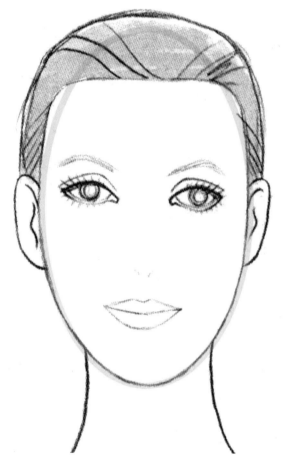

Oval
- soft curves
- curved hairline
- slightly prominent cheekbones

A Woman's Guide to Success: Perfecting Your Professional Image

BODY SHAPES

Women's body shapes are often described by such terms as: a pear, apple, X or H, or some combination. These descriptions try to combine our body shape with figure concerns such as big hips, narrow shoulders, small waist, or no waist. You may have big hips (the apple) but are not very rounded, your hips my be big, but flat. The X shapes indicates a small waist, but does that mean curved hips and bust, big hips and bust or just a small waist? It is much easier to define your body shape first as it relates to the shape of clothing, since we are trying to dress our bodies, and then make minor adjustments to deal with any figure concerns. Let's make it simple and look at two possibilities.

Straight

A body shape that has little or no waist emphasis. Regardless of weight, the hip, rib care and waist project a straighter appearance. This has nothing to do with weight. Some women, regardless of weight, never have a small waist. Their body lines project a straighter line and may be identified as more "athletic" build. (A single extreme characteristic such as a large bust or full hips does not necessarily define a curved body.

Curved

A body line that has definite waist emphasis and soft rounded curves that are well defined. It can be a voluptuous look or just a soft contoured shape that does not appear to be straight. This is not necessarily an overweight body but one that is rounded in shape or stance.

3 Body Lines

Straight

A straight body shape will project some of the following:

- Straight shoulders
- Low bustline
- Prominent collarbones
- Low hip bones
- Wide midriff—thick waist
- Waist, midriff, hip similar in size
- Long torso
- Narrow hip (may have protruding buttocks)
- Flat hips and/or stomach
- Straight legs
- Straight stance
- Straight walk

Remember, a straight bodyline is still feminine. It has a waist, bust, and hip line. The waist may not be small and the hip line is probably not rounded, although it may be broad. Look for an overall shape so that clothing selection will look like it was made for you—like it fits the shape. A round, curved seam will not fit correctly on a straight hip line.

Curved

A curved body shape will project some of the following:

- Soft shoulder line
- High bustline
- Round bust (often full but not necessarily)
- Small or tapered rib cage
- High hip bones
- Roundness of flesh
- Small waist (relative to hip size)
- Round stomach
- Round hip
- Curved legs
- Tilted hip stance
- Hip movement when walking

Remember, a curved body is not necessarily an overweight body. It projects a roundness—a tailored, straight seam does not fit a curved hip properly. It pulls and gaps.

GEOMETRIC SHAPES

Each of these body types have been described with the help of geometric shapes. Face shapes can be considered angular, curved, or some combination of both.

	Angular	**Curved**
Face Shapes	• Square • Rectangle • Diamond • Triangle	• Round • Heart • Pear • Oval • Oblong
Body Shapes	• Triangle • Square • Rectangular	• Ellipse • Oval • Round

3 Body Lines

Now combine the face shapes with the body shapes for the **four bodyline categories**:

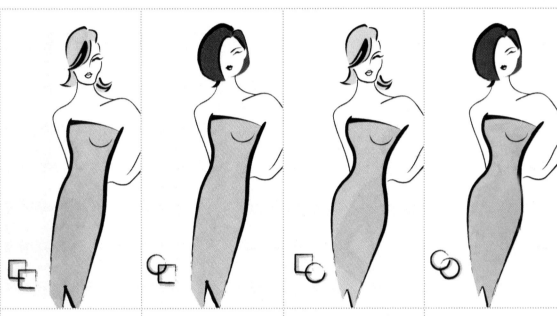

Straight

Angular face shape and straight body line. Body line projects a slightly angular, square, or rectangular shape. Not necessarily thin but with no obvious curves.

Soft-Straight

Curved face shape and straight body line. The general appearance is of a straight body. But because the face projects softness the overall impression projects a softened line on top.

Straight-Soft

An angular face and curved body line. Projects a combination of lines. Straight chiseled features combined with a soft roundness to the body.

Curved

A curved face shape and curved body line. Both the face shape and body line are without the defined straight lines and project roundness and softness.

MATCHING CLOTHING AND BODY LINES

Now that you have determined your body line, you are ready to select clothing that will be a natural extension of your particular body shape. Using this system, your clothing will take on a custom-designed look.

There are two types of lines to consider in selecting clothing shapes: the silhouette line or exterior shape of the garment and the detail lines or the surface lines that affect the overall shape of the garment, including darts, seams, pockets, and shoulder pads.

Fabric and texture also affect the shape and we will discuss these in more details later.

Silhouette Lines

In studying the shape (silhouette) of a suit or garment of clothing, it may be helpful to recall a principle in geometry that defines a line as an infinite number of points with a direction. The direction can either be straight or curved. A shape can be formed with straight lines and angles, curved lines, or a combination. With this as a reference point, let's look at different shapes of women's clothing.

3 Body Lines

Clothing shapes are made with all straight or curved lines or a comination:

1. Made with all straight lines

2. Made with all curved lines

3. Made with straight lines on top and curved on bottom

4, Curved on top and straight on bottom

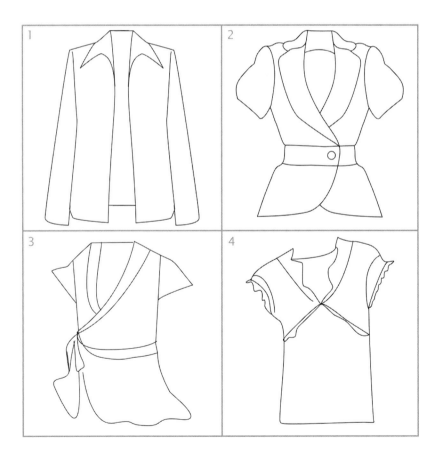

A Woman's Guide to Success:
Perfecting Your Professional Image

WOMEN'S CLOTHING LINES

Selecting clothing to complement your body line:

Straight Clothing Lines

Cividini

Etro

3 Body Lines

Cacheral

Straight Clothing Lines

- Straight silhouettes, little or no shaping in the waist
- A-line dresses and skirts
- Tops with straight side vents, V necklines, notched collars
- Rib knits and stripes
- Geometric patterning
- Pin stripes. checks, and stripes
- Asymmetrical closings
- Tunics and shifts

Herrera

A Woman's Guide to Success:
Perfecting Your Professional Image

Straight Soft Clothing Lines

Ralph Lauren

Versace

3 Body Lines

Straight Soft Clothing Lines

- Shaped and belted jackets
- Waist emphasis
- Notched collars, mandarin necklines, V necks
- Straight lines around face, curved on bottom
- Crisp fabrics on top, soft and flowing on bottom
- Geometrics, stripes and checks on top, floral, paisley, swirls and softness on bottom
- Gently flared skirts
- Trench styles
- Wraps

Badgley & Mischka

Marant

A Woman's Guide to Success:
Perfecting Your Professional Image

Soft Straight Clothing Lines

bcbg

Oscar de la Renta

3 Body Lines

Soft Straight Clothing Lines

- Softness around face
- Straighter lines at body
- Soft knits, cowl necks, rounded collars and lapels
- Shawl collars
- Shifts, tunics, little or no waist emphasis
- Geometrics, plaids, stripes on bottom
- Soft prints, florals, paisleys, swirls on top
- Empire waistlines
- Dropped waists

Hermes

Ralph Lauren

A Woman's Guide to Success:
Perfecting Your Professional Image

Curved Clothing Lines

Oscar

Marc Jacobs

3 Body Lines

Curved Clothing Lines

- Shaped and belted jackets and tops
- Waist emphasis
- Rounded and draped necklines
- Shawl collars, flounces, ruching
- Soft fabrics and patterns, florals, paisleys, swirls
- Plaids on the bias
- Flared or shaped skirts
- Flared and softly pleated slacks

Oscar

Marc Jacobs

ANGULAR

EYEGLASS FRAMES AND HAIRSTYLES FOR DIFFERENT FACE SHAPES

Glasses and hairstyles should complement the shape of your face as your clothing lines complement your body. Avoid extremes: round on round, or square on square, unless looking for a fashion statement. Select a frame with the same or similar line as your face shape but avoid repeating your exact face shape.

Frames should be the same width as your temple. Choose them a little narrower to compensate for a wide face or a little wider for a narrow face.

ANGULAR

Helpful Hints

- Long nose—choose glasses with a low bridge
- Short nose—choose a high, keyhole bridge
- Small or too close together eyes appear wider with a wide or light bridge
- Wide-set eyes appear more balanced with a heavier weight, dark colored bridge

CURVED

CURVED

3 Body Lines

WOMEN'S HAIRSTYLE RECOMMENDATIONS

Angular: Diamond-Shaped Face

- Prominent cheekbones, narrow forehead, pointed chin.
- Emphasize cheekbones with angular hairstyles.
- Add width across your forehead with fullness or bangs.
- Keep hair flat at cheekbones
- Add fullness at chin level

Emphasize your cheekbones with angular hairstyles.

Add width across your forehead with fullness or bangs.

Keep your hair flat at the cheekbones.

Add fullness at chin level.

Angular: Square Face

- Square jawline
- Straight sides
- Emphasize the angles by asymmetrical styles, geometric cuts
- Add height to create balance by adding fullness on top to lengthen face
- Off center part or bangs are suggested
- Add fullness on sides to accent cheek bones

Emphasize your angles with asymmetrical styles or geometric cuts.
Add height to create balance; fullness on top lengthens your face.
Add an off-center part or bangs.
Add fullness on the sides to accent your cheekbones.

3 Body Lines

Angular: Rectangular Face

- Long face shape, square jawline
- Emphasize angles, try asymmetrical styles, geometric cuts
- Shorten length of face with bangs or off-center part
- Add fullness at side to accent cheekbones
- Do not add height or fullness on top

Emphasize your angles by trying asymmetrical styles or
geometric cuts.
Shorten the length of your face with bangs or an off-center part.
Add fullness at the sides to accent your cheekbones.
Do not add height or fullness on top.

Angular: Triangular Face

- Narrow chin, prominent cheekbones, broad forehead
- Emphasize cheekbones with angular hair styles
- Use off center part or bangs to narrow forehead
- Keep hair flat at cheekbones
- Add fullness at chin level

Emphasize your cheekbones with angular hairstyles.
Use off-center part or bangs to make your forehead appear
narrower.
Keep your hair flat at the cheekbones.
Add fullness at chin level.

3 Body Lines

Curved: Round Face

- Soft jawline, soft cheeks, little or no cheekbone definition
- Emphasize curves with soft hairstyles
- Add height to balance neck and face proportions
- Add fullness on top
- Bring hair forward on cheeks to reduce width
- Add asymmetrical focus

Emphasize your curves with soft hairstyles.
Add height to balance your neck and face proportions.
Add fullness on top.
Bring your hair forward on the cheeks to reduce width.
Add asymmetrical focus.

Curved: Heart Face

- Wide forehead, narrow chin
- Emphasize softness and curves
- Use an off-center part to soften and narrow forehead
- Add fullness at chin level

Emphasize your softness and curves.
Use an off-center part to soften and narrow your forehead.
Add fullness at chin level.

3 Body Lines

Curved: Pear Face

- Narrow forehead, full cheeks, and broad chin line
- Emphasize soft curves
- Add fullness and width at forehead to broaden forehead
- Bring hair towards the face at cheek level to narrow cheeks
- Keep hair long enough to soften chin line

Emphasize your soft curves.

Add fullness and width at your forehead to make it appear broader.

Bring your hair toward your face at the cheek level to make your cheeks appear narrower.

Keep your hair long enough to soften your chin line.

Curved: Oval Face

- Soft jawline
- Slight cheekbone emphasis
- Rounded hairline at forehead
- Use softened styles with slight angle for interest

Use softened styles with slight angle for interest.

Marble Bouclé Shaped Coat, Cashmere
Long Sleeve Tie Neck, and Matte Sateen
Single Pleat Pant by Jones New York

A Woman's Guide to Success: Perfecting Your Professional Image

Getting to the top in style—a style that's yours alone—means cutting through the fads and fancies in clothing while developing a natural, custom-designed look. Knowing and understanding your body shape and facial features is a big step toward that goal. You'll make the right choice every time and make your investment wardrobe purchases pay big dividends.

BODY AND FACE CHECKLIST

- Style doesn't change as fashion does. Define your personal style by selecting clothes that are a natural extension of your body line.

- Besides an extension of body line, flattering items need to complement your coloring and personality and fit properly. Seek a balance between line, scale, and color.

- A woman's body can be described as straight or curved. Combining face shapes with the body shapes, we have four women's body lines: straight, soft-straight, straight-soft, and curved.

- Body lines remain fairly constant. Over the years, there may be some shifting and added weight. But for the most part, the body line that defines you now will be the same or similar in the future.

- The lines of clothing can be divided into two: the silhouette line (the exterior shape) and the detail lines.

- Don't fall into the trap of believing in an ideal body shape. You may prefer one, but ultimately any shape can be flattered with the right selection of properly fitted and shaped clothing.

- The shape of your face, like your body, is pretty much set for life. Knowing its geometry will help you achieve consistent style in your clothing, hairstyles, and accessories.

4 Fabrics & Details

A garment's silhouette is a primary definition of line. But there are other ways to make a line straighter or softer. The selection of the fabric type is critical in defining line.

Fabrics that are crisp, stiff, and tightly woven better define straight lines. Using softer fabrics relaxes a silhouette so that it complements the body shape with less exaggerated angles. Patterns and designs in fabrics also make a difference. Stripes, for example, project a straighter line than the swirls. Wool crepe is softer than gabardine. The crisp plaid or check is better for straight lines, and a soft wool challis print produces a softer line.

The details of a garment are touches such as squared or rounded shoulder pads, epaulettes, angled or curved pocket flaps, double breasted jackets, peaked lapels, asymmetrical closings, and well defined darts.

The world of fabrics and details could easily fill many libraries with technical volumes, few of which would be very useful outside the field of custom tailoring and the garment district. However, the following will provide a sampling of the different types of fabrics that are best for the different bodylines.

"My energies are concentrated in my hands when I touch fabric. I think that my constant, almost maniacal research on fabrics is one of the reasons behind my success."

~ Giorgio Armani

A Woman's Guide to Success:
Perfecting Your Professional Image

FOR STRAIGHTER LINES

- Tightly woven
- Gabardine
- Worsted
- Sharkskin
- Linen
- Silk
- Crisp poplin
- Pin stripes
- Crisp Glenn plaids
- Tightly woven herringbones or checks
- Crisp geometric and abstract patterns

Cerruti

Oscar

4 Fabrics & Details

Valentino

Balenciaga

A Woman's Guide to Success:
Perfecting Your Professional Image

SOFTER FABRICS

- Softly woven
- Tweeds
- Wool flannel
- Nubby textures
- Cashmere
- Matte finishes, patterns and designs that contain paisleys, swirls, blended stripes

Valentino   Anna Sui

4 Fabrics & Details

Rykiel

Nina Ricci

A Woman's Guide to Success:
Perfecting Your Professional Image

HOW FABRIC WEIGHT AND TEXTURE AFFECT THE CHARACTER OF A GARMENT

4 Fabrics & Details

BONE STRUCTURE AND YOUR FACIAL FEATURES

Facial characteristics are defined differently. Cheeks, nose shapes, lips, and chin sizes are described as broad, average, or fine.

These terms are critical to making successful clothing choices.

The words carry no subjective or judgmental overtones. They are used to determine which fabrics and details go best with your shape and style to give you a balanced appearance. This is how it works.

Large bones, broad facial features: Select heavier-weight fabrics, accessories, and eyeglass frames. The lighter weights make it appear as if you overpower your clothing.

Small bones, average facial features: Stay away from heavy fabrics, frames, and accessories. Your clothes will overpower you.

Look at the drawings of the two different jackets in the chart entitled "How Fabric Weight Affects The Character of a Garment." You will notice that one of them is drawn with a fine tipped pen, indicating a lighter weight fabric. The other is drawn with a broad tipped pen, indicating a heavier look that would be more balanced on someone with larger bone structure.

Fabrics come in all weights. It is only necessary to look and feel the materials to recognize the differences. To be aware of such details helps clue you in as to why you may have been more comfortable with certain things in your closet.

FABRIC AND YOUR BONE STRUCTURE

Your bone structure and the way the muscle and flesh is arranged around your bones define your body and facial characteristics. The structure may be large, small or in between. How do you know for sure where you fit in?

Look at your wrists, ankles, fingers. You will be able to compare the circumferences with standard items like watch bands, rings, cuffs, and shoes. For those with larger bone structure, once again, select heavier weight fabrics and accessories. For those with smaller, fine, or delicate bone size and features, look for less weight for balance and harmony.

The following chart will help you determine whether you have small, medium, or large bones and facial features.

YOUR BONE STRUCTURE		
	Wrist	**Ankle**
Small Bones	5½" (14 cm) or less	8" (20 cm) or less
Medium Bones	5½—6" (14—16.5 cm)	8—9" (20—23 cm)
Large Bones	6" (16.5 cm) & over	9" (23 cm) & over

Remember that bone structure must be considered in relation to your overall size. What is small for one person may be average for a shorter person. This chart is for those of average height.

4 Fabrics & Details

THE BEST FABRICS FOR BUSINESSWEAR

While there isn't an absolute rule about which fabrics fit in best on the job, certain unspoken traditions have evolved. These have mostly to do with the look and feel projected by certain fabrics and blends. Perhaps the most obvious aspect is that some fabrics have a "richer" look than others; in a quiet way they have an "executive" aura.

The most recommended for a business setting are 100 percent wool, wool blends, cotton, cotton blends, silks, and linen blends. Linen is a beautiful natural fabric but because of its tendency to wrinkle so badly, it is better left for more casual wear. Very shiny fabrics are also not recommended.

"I base most of my fashion taste on what doesn't itch."

~ Gilda Radner

It is generally agreed that the best blends are 55 percent or more of natural fibers and 45 percent or less of man-made fiber. In the past, only natural fibers were recommended for serious suits and other basic investment pieces. These days, there are some who still prefer these quality fabrics. However, progress has been made in the quality of synthetics and there are excellent blends available to the general market.

"Luxury must be comfortable, otherwise it is not luxury."

~ Coco Chanel

It has become a matter of personal choice. Natural materials are cooler in warm weather, and some prefer the feel. Others like blends because they are easier to care for and in some cases, such as linen, wrinkle less. Either way, comfort and fit are important considerations.

COMBINING PRINTS AND PATTERNS

Mixing patterns and prints, when done well, creates a fun, fashion forward, and often a sophisticated look. There are a few guidelines that can be followed for a successful creation. The colors in both prints should be the same or a related color carried through in both. The prints should be of different scale. Combining a small foulard print with a stripe works well. A large floral print works with a check or plaid in the same coloration.

Although mixing of patterns and prints subtly done is acceptable for conservative looks, like combining a small print blouse with a stripe or check suit, avoid more elaborate combinations in the workplace. Save these combinations for leisure or dressy looks unless you are very experienced in creating these special looks.

1. Floral patterns and appliqués
2. Lace and beading
3. Contrasting trim and piping, decorative buttons
4. Lace trim, button details
5. Mixes of patterns and texture, fringe, and appliqués
6. Crisp, tightly woven fabrics
7. Abstract patterns
8. Contrasting bias detail, mix of shiny and knit fabrications

1. Floral Turtleneck & Skirt by Etro
2. Lace Blouse & Beaded Check Skirt by Beth Bowley
3. Shell-Button Jacket & Floral-Print Skirt by Moschino Cheap & Chic
4. Twinset & Plaid Skirt by Blumarine
5. Plaid Jacket, Dancers Turtleneck & Tweed Skirt by Moschino Cheap & Chic
6. Plaid Suit by Kay Unger New York
7. Printed Twinset by NM Exclusive
8. Striped Sweater & Skirt by Marc Jacobs

4 Fabrics & Details

Marled Bouclé Back Belted Jacket, 3/4 Sleeve V-Neck Silk Knit & Ottoman Seamed Skirt by Jones New York

4 Fabrics & Details

Fabrics and details are critical to complementing body and face shapes, emphasizing straight and more contoured or curved lines, as required. This list provides the summary data you need to make smart choices.

FABRICS & PATTERNS CHECKLIST

- For straight lines, think fabrics that are crisp, stiff, and tightly woven. Contoured or curved lines are complemented with soft, fine, or loosely woven fabrics.

- As fabric selections are softened, shoulder treatment, pocket styles, darts, and other details are softened.

- Patterns and prints also make a difference in lines. The stripe, for example, projects a straighter line than the paisley.

- Proper combining of patterns and prints creates the finishing touch for a pulled together look.

- Continuity in fabric, line, print, and design needs to be maintained. Lines should work together. You needn't match everything, but be sure there is a relationship between the lines of each element.

- Check your bone structure and determine if it is large, medium, or small. See if your facial features are broad, average, or fine. Balance fabric, details, and accessories to achieve balance and harmony.

- Fabric texture is also a function of body and facial structure. Lighter and finer textures are better for smaller body sizes. Medium to heavy textures are better for those who are taller and bigger.

- For businesswear, the most accepted fabrics are 100 percent natural fibers. The best blends are 55 percent natural.

5 Fit & Quality

ONLY GREAT WILL DO

It is called "scale"—fitting clothes perfectly to your shape. It is the cut that, in all details, looks like it was made for you.

Scale is the essential difference between looking ordinary and elegant. Not foppish elegance, but quiet good taste. It is amazing that this #10 secret of dressing well isn't universally known. Fit—fit and good materials. If you achieve it, what you get is consistency, quality, simplicity, and comfort. Elegance.

Warning: Fit has its downside.

If you insist on being tightly fitted, you will be inelegant.

Most custom tailored suits fit the body in an easy, natural way. There is plenty of room to move around in, perfect for your body and shape, without being overly loose. This gives an expensive look. If you are thin, this cut will make you look heavier. And if you are heavy, it will make you look 10 pounds lighter.

Bodies change and proper fitting requires that you take all the time necessary to try on and get it fitted right. Women know that depending on the brand, season, and fashion direction, sizes mean nothing. A size 6 in one season can mean a 10 the next with no weight gain. That is a problem with women's fashion. Even in a season of "clingy" and tight fitting, tight is never appropriate for the workplace.

"We must never confuse elegance with snobbery."

~ Yves Saint Laurent

A Woman's Guide to Success:
Perfecting Your Professional Image

FIT & QUALITY CHECKPOINTS:

- **Price isn't everything, especially when it comes to the right fit.** No matter how much you pay for an item of clothing, if the fit isn't there, then everything else suffers. Poor fit makes a $1000 suit look cheap, and the highest quality will seem shoddy.

- Most fine stores employ one or more tailors, but it's up to you to understand the possibilities you see reflected in the fitting room mirror. **It is best if you can communicate with the tailor and, to some extent, guide the tailoring process.**

What follows are basics in good fit and quality construction and some tips on how to adjust your clothing choices to solve minor proportion concerns.

> *"Fashion is architecture: it is a matter of proportions."*
>
> ~ Coco Chanel

> *"I'm nothing to look at, so the only thing I can do is dress better than anyone else."*
>
> ~ Wallis Simpson, Duchess of Windsor

5 Fit & Quality

FIT AND QUALITY CONSTRUCTION

Proper Fit: Blouse

- **Set-in sleeve:** Reach for shoulder bone or top of shoulder; seam should be just outside of shoulder bone (approx. 1".)

- **Sleeve length:** Should be at wrist bone.

- **Sleeve width:** There should be at least 1½" of double fabric when you reach up and pinch the sleeve away from your upper arm.

- **Buttons:** Must remain closed with at least 1" of fabric on each side of bustline.

- **Midriff:** There should be 2" of double fabric as you reach up and pinch the fabric from each side (this will allow for proper blousing.)

- **Length:** Should be no shorter than hip bone.

FIT AND QUALITY CONSTRUCTION

Proper Fit: Skirt

- **Pleats:** Should never pull open. There should be no crease or pull across break of leg.

- **Pockets:** Must remain closed and should not pull open.

- **Straight skirts:** Should hang from buttocks in a straight line and not curve under.

- **Skirt:** Should not ride up when you sit.

- **Hip line:** There should be at least 1" of extra fabric when you pull the skirt from your body at hip line.

- **Waistband:** Should be loose enough to allow for two fingers to be inserted.

- **Thighs:** Must not show; you should be able to easily turn your skirt around your body.

- **Panty line:** Must not show.

5 Fit & Quality

FIT AND QUALITY CONSTRUCTION

Proper Fit: Jacket

- **Shoulder:** Should be at least 1" wider than shoulder bone.

- **Collar:** Must not wrinkle across back.

- **When buttoned:** The coat should allow for sweater or blouse and still not pull across shoulder or hip. There should be 1½" of extra fabric at midriff.

- **Sleeve length:** Should allow for ½ to ¼" of blouse sleeve to show.

- **Sleeve width:** Should allow for blouse or sweater, and still have ½" of extra fabric.

- **Back:** There should be no pull across back.

- **Pockets:** Must remain closed; any pleat or dart must lie flat.

NOTE: Jacket, skirt, and slack lengths will be covered later.

FIT AND QUALITY CONSTRUCTION

Proper Fit: Slacks

- **Pleats:** Must remain closed.

- **Zippers and closings:** Must lie flat.

- **Pant leg:** Should fall straight from hip with no curve under at buttocks.

- **Pockets:** Should not gape or pull open.

- **Hip:** There must be at least 1 to 1½" of fabric when you pull the fabric from your hip bone.

- **Waist:** Should be loose enough to allow for two fingers to be inserted.

- **Panty line:** Must not show.

FIT AND QUALITY CONSTRUCTION
Quality Construction

Seams

- Inside seam allowance should be at least 5/8"
- Seams should be finished with zig-zag or clean finish
- Seam line should not pull or wrinkle but should "hang straight"
- No thread should be loose
- Exterior stitching should be even, straight with no loose threads

Interfacing and facings

- Should not wrinkle, gape or pull
- Should be sewn in rather than fused
- Inside facings should have top-stitching or be on the bias

Hemlines

- Must hang evenly and straight
- Must be finished with tape or clean finished on edge
- Stitching must be loose and should not pull
- Stitching should not be visible

Pockets

- Must be straight
- Must be clean finished
- Must lie flat

Vintage Inspired 3-Piece Wardrober
by George Simonton Collection

SOLUTIONS FOR MINOR FIGURE CONCERNS: **Broad Shoulders**

Wear
• Small shoulder pads
• V or scoop neck
• Halters
• Raglan or dolman sleeves
• Long necklaces and scarves
• Hip interest to balance shoulders

Avoid
• Epaulets
• Details at shoulder
• Boat necklines
• Wide shoulder pads

1. Luxe V-Neck Top by Juicy Couture
2. Gathered Halter Dress by NM Exclusive
3. Halter Top by Elie Tahari
4. Sweater by Anne Klein
5. Knitted Dress & Scarf by Eileen Fisher
6. Printed Dress by Vivienne Tam

5 Fit & Quality

SOLUTIONS FOR MINOR FIGURE CONCERNS: **Narrow Shoulders**

Wear
- Shoulder pads to extend shoulders
- Cap sleeves
- Boat necks
- Horizontal details at shoulders
- Dropped shoulder seams
- Wide scoop necklines
- Gathers at shoulders
- Wide lapels, softly shaped
- Brooch set up towards shoulder

Avoid
- Raglan or dolman sleeves
- Low V necklines
- Halter necklines

1. Off-the-Shoulder Sweater by Moschino Cheap & Chic
2. Cutout Turtleneck by Jean Paul Gaultier
3. Printed Blazer by Emilio Pucci
4. Clutch Coat by Donna Karan Collection
5. Jeweled Sweater by NM Exclusive
6. Striped Top by NM Exclusive

SOLUTIONS FOR MINOR FIGURE CONCERNS: **Short Legs**

Wear
• Short skirts
• High waistline skirts and slacks
• Cropped trousers
• Pantyhose to match shoe and hemline
• Medium heels

Avoid
• Border designs at hemline
• Long, pleated skirts
• Cuffs on trousers or gathered at ankles
• Very high or very flat heels

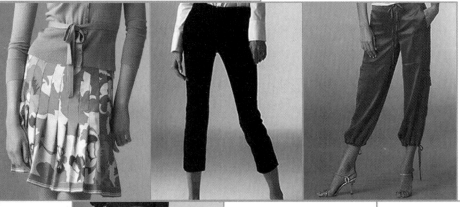

1. Cardigan & Pleated Skirt by Elie Tahari
2. Velvet Capris by Piazza Sempione
3. Cargo Capris by Dana Buchman
4. Sweater & Pants by NM Exclusive
5. "Carmen" Pump by Kors Michael Kors

5 Fit & Quality

SOLUTIONS FOR MINOR FIGURE CONCERNS: **Long Legs**

Wear
- Short skirts at or below knee
- Long, pleated skirts
- Cuffs on trousers
- Interest at leg area using pleats and border designs
- Dropped yokes
- Flared trousers

Avoid
- Very short skirts
- Cropped trousers
- High waistline skirts and slacks

1. Cashmere Jacket & Crepe Pants by Anne Klein
2. Cashmere Sweater, Suede Belt & Paisley Skirt by Ralph Lauren Black Label
3. Cropped Jacket & Pleated Skirt by Burberry
4. Donegal Tweed Mule by Prada
5. Cardigan & Pants by Nanette Lepore

SOLUTIONS FOR MINOR FIGURE CONCERNS: **Narrow Hips**

Wear
▪ Pleated trousers and skirts
▪ Pockets and details at hip level
▪ Jacket that ends at hip level
▪ Small shoulder pads
▪ Patterns and prints on bottom
▪ Solid tops

Avoid
▪ Pencil slim skirts
▪ Center seam on skirts
▪ Dark colors on bottom
▪ Large shoulder pads
▪ Tight trousers

1. Crochet Cardigan &
   Pleated Skirt by Kay Unger
2. Patchwork Blazer &
   Paisley Skirt by Etro
3. Suit by Valentino
4. Flannel Suit by
   NM Exclusive
5. Painted Pocket Jeans by
   7 For All Mankind

5 Fit & Quality

SOLUTIONS FOR MINOR FIGURE CONCERNS: **Large Hips**

Wear
• Long tops ending below or above hip
• Chemise styles
• Dropped belt
• Stitched-down pleats
• Center seams, inverted pleats
• Solid, deep colors on bottom
• Prints or bright colors on top
• Vertical stripes
• Shoulder pads to balance hips
• Loose, pleated trouser
• Long shorts or culottes

Avoid
• Pockets and details at hipline
• Jackets and tops that end at widest part of hip
• Prints or patterns on bottom
• Light colors on bottom
• Shoulder bags at hip level
• Short, pleated skirts and shorts
• Tight belts

1. Striped Shirt by Burberry
2. Chiffon Top & Cropped Pants by BCBG Maxazria
3. Floral Tee & Pleated Skirt by Prada Sport
4. Plaid Jacket and Pants by Ellen Tracy
5. Piped Shirt & Pants by Go Silk

SOLUTIONS FOR MINOR FIGURE CONCERNS: **Small Bust**

Wear
<ul><li>Textures and layering</li><li>Horizontal lines at bustline</li><li>Design detail at bustline</li><li>Pockets at bustline</li><li>Loose fitting garments</li><li>Bows and draped collars</li><li>Cowl necks</li><li>Gathers at bustline for fullness</li><li>Embroidery and soft details at bustline</li><li>Yokes</li><li>High waisted skirts/trousers with fuller top</li></ul>

Avoid
<ul><li>Low necklines unless accompanied by scarves or jewelry</li><li>Tight fitting tops</li></ul>

1. Textured Jacket & Skirt by Anna Sui
2. Sweater with Tie by TSE Cashmere
3. Embroidered Jacket & Dress by Shoshanna
4. Cowl Neck Top & Skirt by Eskandar
5. Bow Cardigan by Nanette Lepore

5 Fit & Quality

SOLUTIONS FOR MINOR FIGURE CONCERNS: **Large Bust**

Wear	Avoid
<ul><li>V or Scoop necklines</li><li>Open necklines with shawl, collars, or curved lapels</li><li>Long sleeves</li><li>Dolman sleeves</li><li>Loose fitting garments</li><li>Vertical details</li><li>Dropped waist garments</li><li>Low slung belts</li><li>Solid colors on top</li></ul>	<ul><li>Tight fitting tops</li><li>Textures</li><li>Pockets at bustline</li><li>High waisted skirts/trousers with fuller top</li></ul>

1. Striped Sweater by NM Exclusive
2. Top by DKNY
3. Cardigan & Superfine Tee by NM Exclusive
4. Luxe Suit by Ellen Tracy
5. Twist-Neck Dress by David Meister

SOLUTIONS FOR MINOR FIGURE CONCERNS: **Long Waist**

Wear
• Empire and high rise waist
• Wide belts
• Belts the same color as bottoms
• Over blouses
• Blouses tied at waist

Avoid
• Short tops
• Narrow belts
• Drop waist styles
• No waistbands

1. Empire-Waist Dress by Kay Unger New York
2. Lace Blouse & Skirt by Chetta B
3. Sleeveless Sweater & Boucle Skirt by Milly
4. Cashmere Cardigan & Twill Pants by Ellen Tracy
5. Paisley Suit by Ellen Tracy

5 Fit & Quality

SOLUTIONS FOR MINOR FIGURE CONCERNS: **Short Waist**

Wear	Avoid
• Yokes on skirts • Medium to narrow belts • Dropped waist • Hip focus • No waistband • Belts the same color as tops • Low slung belts • Over blouses	• Wide waistband and belts • Contrasting belts

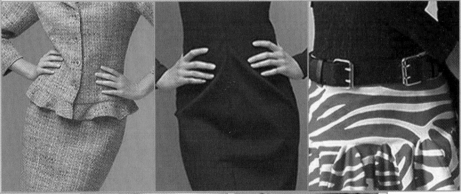

1. Ruffled Jacket & Skirt by NM Exclusive
2. Zip-Front Dress by Narciso Rodriguez
3. City-Print Turtleneck & Zebra-Print Skirt by Moschino Jeans
4. Tie Jacket by Ilana Wolf
5. Tunic & Easy Trousers by Joan Vass

SOLUTIONS FOR MINOR FIGURE CONCERNS: **Long Neck**

Wear
• Scarves tied at neckline
• Necklines with bows, gathers, and ruffles
• Necklaces with curved lines
• Choker necklaces
• Rolled high collars
• Upturned collars
• Cowl necks

Avoid
• Low necklines unless accompanied by scarves or jewelry
• Very short hairstyle

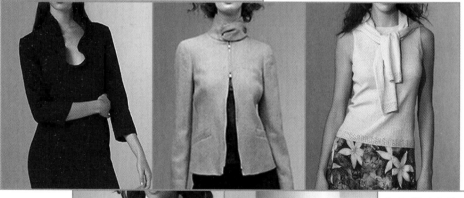

1. Ruffled-Collar Dress by Valentino Roma
2. Scarf-Neck Jacket & Pants by Armani Collezioni
3. Twinset & Orchid Skirt by Anne Klein
4. Chenille Poncho & Sash Pants by Cynthia Steffe
5. Quartz & Pearl Choker by Lenni Navarro

5 Fit & Quality

SOLUTIONS FOR MINOR FIGURE CONCERNS: **Short Neck**

Wear	Avoid
• V or scooped necklines • Open collars • Bows and scarves tied low • Long necklaces • Short hairstyles	• High neck treatments • Large necklaces and chokers • Scarves tied high at neck • Upturned collars

1. Cashmere V-Neck by Juicy Couture
2. Stretch Pinstriped Suit by Anne Klein
3. Corduroy Shirt & Striped Pants by Company by Ellen Tracy
4. Multistrand Pearl Necklace by David Yurman
5. Tweed Suit & Blouse by Teri Jon

SOLUTIONS FOR MINOR FIGURE CONCERNS: **Tall (5'9" and over)**

Wear
• Horizontal designs
• Layered clothing
• Wide contrasting dropped belts
• Contrasting bands of color
• Designs at hemline
• Full hairstyle
• Wide hats

Avoid
• Vertical lines
• Deep necklines
• Dressing in one color
• Long shoulder bags and scarves
• Small accessories

1. Floral Dress & Scarf by Harari
2. One-Shoulder Top & Skirt by Donna Karan Collection
3. Zip Poncho by Burberry
4. Cherry Dress by Marc Jacobs
5. Chain-Lace Dress & Conch Belt by Michael Kors

5 Fit & Quality

SOLUTIONS FOR MINOR FIGURE CONCERNS: **Petite (small bone, 5'2" & under)**

Wear
- Vertical designs and lines
- Uncluttered styles
- Toned tops and bottoms
- Medium to lightweight fabrics
- Medium to small patterns
- Medium to little textures
- Medium to small accessories

Avoid
- Wide and bulky garments
- Too much volume in hair
- Heavy texture
- Heavy accessories and shoes

1. Tweed Jacket & Skirt by Philosophy di Alberta Ferretti
2. Pinstriped Suit by Tahari
3. Hoodie & Capris by Eileen Fisher
4. Quilted Vest & Trousers by Eileen Fisher
5. Pique Dress by Lacoste

SOLUTIONS FOR MINOR FIGURE CONCERNS: **Underweight**

Wear
<ul><li>Horizontal lines/seams</li><li>Loosely constructed clothing</li><li>Textured fabric</li><li>Pleats on trousers and skirts</li><li>3/4 or long sleeve</li><li>Layered clothing</li></ul>

Avoid
<ul><li>Vertical lines/seams</li><li>Tight trousers and skirts</li><li>Very long hair</li><li>Heavy shoes</li><li>Long necklaces</li><li>Long necklines</li><li>Tight clothing</li></ul>

1. Striped Turtleneck & Scarf by Joan Vass
2. Boucle Suit by Teri Jon
3. Floral Jacket & Pleated Skirt by Jon
4. Crocheted Top & Pleated Skirt by D&G Dolce & Gabbana
5. Pleated Blouse by Kay Unger New York

5 Fit & Quality

SOLUTIONS FOR MINOR FIGURE CONCERNS: **Overweight**

Wear	Avoid
<ul><li>Medium to large scale accessories</li><li>Toned hose and shoes in darker shade</li><li>Medium to large scale prints</li><li>Vertical or diagonal style lines</li><li>Loose fitting clothing</li></ul>	<ul><li>Horizontal lines</li><li>Small accessories and prints</li><li>Too many colors</li><li>Too short hairstyle</li><li>Delicate shoes</li></ul>

1. Dress by Joan Vass
2. Oversized Top & Easy Trousers by Joan Vass
3. Tailored Sweater Jacket, Shell & Pants Joan Vass
4. Cashmere Cardigan & Shell by TSE Cashmere
5. Pinstripe Suit & Shirt by Dana Buchman

Wool Blend Long Sleeve Argyle Crewneck & Dressy Stretch Angle Pocket Pant by Jones New York

5 Fit & Quality

FIT & QUALITY CHECKLIST:

- When considering the purchase of expensive outfits, it is best to have all the information and tips on hand. **You may want to take this checklist with you on your next foray to the store.**

- **Scale**—the fitting of clothes to your particular body shape—is the difference between looking super and ordinary—or less. Your best bet is a loose (not baggy) fit. **Stay away from tight body clinging fits.**

- **Go with your current vital statistics.** Chances are that last year's measurements may have changed. Be aware of this when choosing the size to try on.

- Carefully look at the shape and proportion of the garment and choose the one that best reflects your body shape. **Remember you can't put a round peg into a square hole.**

- Look at the fabric and be sure that it is not too stiff or loosely woven for your shape.

- Look for patterns and prints that are harmonious with your clothing and body lines.

- When trying on clothing, bring the shoes and other items you plan to wear with the items.

- **Check for proper fit!**

SHOPPING GUIDELINES:

Go with a Plan

- Use your priority shopping list and avoid impulse buying.

- When buying a suit, the most expensive item in your wardrobe, get the best quality within your price range. Before you make a purchase, try an expensive suit in your right line to get an idea of how it looks and feels, look at the tailoring, fabric, the details. When trying on a similar, less expensive, suit, the quality, fabric, and fit should be your main concerns.

- When updating your wardrobe, purchase a few of the new seasonal colors and patterns in sweaters, scarves, blouses, and accessories.

- Beware of special purchase items. Sometimes they are not up to the regular quality of the store merchandise.

- When buying sale items, check the quality and be sure the items are on your "to get list."

- When buying accessories, such as shoes, handbags, or briefcases, do not compromise on quality. Good accessories can make or break your look.

- When buying a suit wear the top, blouse, shoes, and accessories you plan to wear with it.

6 Personal Style

WHAT'S PERFECT FOR YOU

"Simplicity is the keynote to all true elegance..."

~ Coco Chanel

"A woman is closest to being naked when she is well dressed"

~ Coco Chanel

It is time to put everything in order using the information and insight you have gained from the previous chapters.

In this chapter, we have matched body lines with clothing lines and put together a list of things to look for with respect to detail, fabric, and accessories. Use these charts as a reference. Compare the other body types and related clothing lines and fabrics to better understand those that will work for you and how to add selections from other charts so that you will maintain your personal style, one that reflects who you are from the inside out.

Face and Body Shapes				
	Straight	**Curved face, straight body**	**Angular face, curved body**	**Curved face, curved body**
Face Shape	Square, Rectangle, Diamond, Triangle	Oval, Ellipse	Square, Soft Edges on Square or Rectangle	Round, Oval
Body Shape	Inverted Triangle (Broad Shoulders) Rectangle, square, or some combination with the Triangle	Rectangle with Slight Curve	Ellipse	Oval or Round
Overall	Angular Face, Straight Body	Ellipse with the slight beginning of a curve	Ellipse, slightly rounded, curved	Round, very curved, voluptuous body

STRAIGHT:

Angular face ▪
Straight body

Straight Silhouette Lines

- Crisp, straight closing
- Angular and asymmetrical detail
- Well-defined shoulders
- Straight jacket and skirt hemline
- Little or no waist emphasis
- Tailored lines

Straight Details

It is important for the details used on clothing to be consistent with the silhouette lines.

Darts:	Long straight, sharply defined or no darts.
Seams:	Well-defined seam lines, top-stitching, contrasting piping, braid, or trim.
Pleats:	Pressed-down, stitched-down, asymmetrical, unpressed pleats.
Sleeves:	Set-in, straight pleats at shoulder, square shoulder pads, tapered sleeves, crisp puffs.
Lapels:	Notched, pointed, peaked, or no lapels, edge-to-edge.
Collars:	Angled, crisp, straight.
Pockets:	Well-defined, square, piped, slashed.
Necklines:	Square, boat, jewel, contrasting trim, V, mandarin, turtleneck.
Fabrics:	Tightly woven fabrics, little or no texture.
Accessories:	Choose angular shapes scaled to your body size and bone structure.
Eyeglass Frames:	Choose frames with some straightness across the top or with squared edges to complement the angles in your face.

6 Personal Style

Discover or confirm your bodyline and find the seasonal wardrobe, eyeglass frame, and styles to complement your personal style. Become a member at www.alwaysinstyle.com and complete the bodyline profile.

SOFT-STRAIGHT:

Contoured face ▪ Straight body

Soft-Straight Silhouette Lines

- Combination of straight and smooth lines
- Soft lines around face
    - Straighter silhouettes below bustline
    - Unconstructed shapes that are neither all straight nor all curved

Soft-Straight Details

It is important for the details used on clothing to be consistent with the silhouette lines.

Darts:	Use in combination with eased detail.
Seams:	Straight with unconstructed look; self-top-stitching works well.
Pleats:	Pressed-down with soft fabric, unpressed.
Sleeves:	Set-in, raglan, dolman, rounded shoulder pads.
Lapels:	Notched with round edges, notched soft fabric, shawl, bias, no lapel with curved closing, rounded, dropped notch.
Collars:	Rolled, cowl, notched with rounded corners.
Pockets:	Patch with round bottoms, flap.
Necklines:	Curved, scoop, cowl, draped, ruffled, jewel.
Fabrics:	Soft woven fabric, medium to maximum texture.
Accessories:	Choose curved shapes around face scaled to your body size and bone structure. Choose softened geometric shapes, unconstructed or constructed of soft material.
Eyeglass Frames:	Choose frames with round or curved edges to complement the curves in your face.

STRAIGHT-SOFT:

Angular face ▪
Curved body

Straight-Soft Silhouette Lines

- Combination of straight and smooth lines
- Crisp, straight lines around face and shoulders
- Waist emphasis
- Unconstructed and wrap shapes that are neither all straight nor all curved

Straight-Soft Details

It is important for the details used on clothing to be consistent with the silhouette lines.

Darts:	Soft gathers, soft pleats, eased, used in combination with straight details.
Seams:	Straight with shaping at or below waist.
Pleats:	Soft, unpressed, gathered, eased.
Sleeves:	Set-in, squared-off pads or pleated detail.
Lapels:	Notched or peaked with soft fabric, no lapels.
Collars:	Notched, pointed, stand-up straight.
Pockets:	Slashed, flap, square with soft fabric.
Necklines:	Boat, jewel, V, mandarin, turtleneck.
Fabrics:	Soft woven fabric, medium to maximum texture.
Accessories:	Choose angular shapes around face scaled to your body size and bone structure.
Eyeglass Frames:	Choose frames with some straightness across the top to complement the angles in your face.

6 Personal Style

Discover or confirm your bodyline and find the seasonal wardrobe, eyeglass frame, and styles to complement your personal style. Become a member at www.alwaysinstyle.com and complete the bodyline profile.

CURVED:

Contoured face ▪ Curved body

Curved Silhouette Lines
- Smooth, sleek curves on closing and lapels
- Soft skirts
  - Rounded hemline
  - Eased, flowing with movement to fall with the curves, not against them

Curved Details

It is important for the details used on clothing to be consistent with the silhouette lines.

Darts:	Soft gathers, soft pleats, eased.
Seams:	Curved seams, no top-stitching, or fine top-stitching, eased.
Pleats:	Soft, unpressed, gathered.
Sleeves:	Gathered, drop-shoulder, raglan, dolman, full and billowy.
Lapels:	Rounded, curved, shawl, bias, no lapels with curved closing.
Collars:	Round, rolled, cowl, notched with rounded edges or drop notch.
Pockets:	Flap, rounded, set-in.
Necklines:	Round, scoop, cowl, draped, ruffled, jewel, flounced.
Fabrics:	Soft woven fabric and patterns. Little or no texture.
Accessories:	Choose curved shapes scaled to your body size and bone structure.
Eyeglass Frames:	Choose frames with round or curved edges to complement the curves in your face.

Part 2

Color

Wearing the right colors is an art and a science, both of which are easy and exciting to master.

The first thing to understand is that color, like clothing lines and styles, needs to be individualized; it has to be as personal a choice as selecting the right cut and fabric for your particular body shape. The same four rules apply that have been generalized in the description of the well-dressed person. Colors must complement you physically, express your personality, must be appropriate for the occasion, and the use and combinations must be current.

It would be wonderful if we could simply wear the colors that appeal to us the most at all times. You can do that, of course, if you're one of those lucky people with a flawlessly innate sense of what works and what doesn't. But for most of us, it's a matter of learning the rules, and that's what this section is all about. Color—one of the most critically important elements of personal style—is the first order of business in this section on Successful Style.

Because color is probably the most subjective and least understood facet of dress, we've reduced (if not eliminated) the guess work with a simple, easy to follow series of charts. Once you discover which color chart describes you best, you will always be able to make the correct picks, and mixing and matching will help expand your present wardrobe.

7 | Color at Work

HOW TO MAKE IT WORK FOR YOU

Wearing the right color can brighten your whole appearance. It can create mood, individuality—even power. Dark colors, for example, project strength and authority. Have you ever noticed that many successful male attorneys plead their cases in dark suits, crisp white shirt, and sober-looking neckties? He might wear a light gray or tan suit, blue shirt, and more colorful tie for a more approachable, friendly look. Women create a more powerful effect with dark neutral suits, conservative blouses, and lots of contrast. On the other hand, women who want to affect a lighter, less serious look might wear a light gray, pastel, or fashion color. More color, print, and pattern, or less contrast is less powerful.

"Colors, like features, follow the changes of the emotions."

~ Pablo Picasso

"All colors are the friends of their neighbors and the lovers of their opposites."

~ Marc Chagall

All of this occurs in the eye of the beholder; it is totally subjective, neither positive nor negative. It is true that there is a general consensus of opinion on the psychological aspects of color and its effect in general. These are the facts we are working with along with our own professional opinions. But think for a moment: As an attorney defending a client facing a serious charge, which colors would you choose for the courtroom? Dark, of course, as we mentioned above. Just how dark to maintain the appearance of power, your power, and not let the color overpower you, will be discussed in the next section. It will, of course, depend on your personal color characteristics as your clothing line selection depends on your face and body shape.

The choice of the courtroom suit will not affect the cause of justice except the judge and jurors will be more inclined to notice you and pay slightly closer attention to your words, if you are presenting a powerful look without being overpowering.

STRICTLY FOR LOOKS

We will return to the "power" aspect of color later in this chapter. For now, let's concentrate on the ways color can make you look terrific all of the time.

Wearing the right colors enhances your complexion. Lines and wrinkles seen to disappear, circles under the eyes are less obvious; you take on a visible glow. This can often be seen with renewed color in the cheeks and skin tone. For men, the "five o'clock shadow" will often seem less obvious since complementary colors cause less shadowing on the face.

The end product of such enhancement creates a younger, more relaxed, appearance. If you are young anyway, you will look as if you have put in a few overtime sessions at the health club.

The right colors also enhance your eyes. Proper color combinations make your eyes brighter, more attentive-looking. Eye contact, as important in business as in the bedroom, is noticeably magnified when your colors are right. You gain credibility and trust. Complementary colors add harmony and balance to your appearance and invest real value in what you are wearing.

The bottom line is this. Color is the final, and perhaps most visible, element of looking good. It's the finishing all important touch that makes the line and scale work.

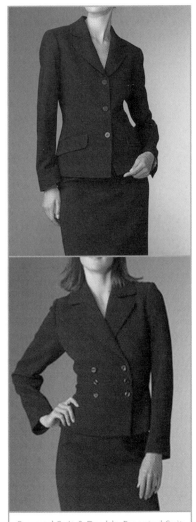

Seamed Suit & Double-Breasted Suit by Tahari

7 Color at Work

THE POWER FACTOR AND MORE

Color conveys power. It also conveys other messages.

If you are not entirely convinced by the example of the attorney in the courtroom, think about how color is shrewdly used in product development.

Start in your own kitchen. Your refrigerator and most appliances are white or pale shades of other colors. The idea is to convey the notion of spic-and-span orderliness. As the fashion colors change new colors start to convey a "new updated" decor. Almond color appliances appeared a few years ago to replace the avocado green and gold. As gourmet cooking became more popular, many switched to stainless steel, the professional look used in restaurant kitchens by professional cooks.

Just as color helps change the mood of the room, it creates indications of type of use expected in that room and very importantly sets a date—how current, how new, how fashionable, what era—much the same way our styles of clothes project a date. With color as with line, detail, and style in general, we must update, or the message sent to others says, "I'm behind."

Flannel Suit by NM Exclusive
Melange Pant Suit by Tahari

A Woman's Guide to Success: Perfecting Your Professional Image

There are many products that are less affected by current changes in fashion trends, but their success still depends on hidden messages in the packages. Flat gun-metal blue for men's electric razors and tools is a typical hi-tech hue that says power, reliability, and function.

Out on the street you will notice that your local policeman's uniform is either paramilitary brown, navy, or flat black. These shades say law and order, authority, raw power. Ask yourself how seriously you would take a policeman in an all white uniform in New York City. The answer is not very! Naval officers wear "dress whites," but at sea the military hues are the order of the day, and that means dark or khaki colors. In other parts of the world, especially tropical countries, white may be used for climate and/or cultural reasons. Any cultural use of color has its own built-in message, more strong than any that is learned directly.

The same messages apply in the corporate world. Navy and gray are the classic order of the day for men. Black suits should be reserved for more formal attire for men. Women can add black to their gray and navy for corporate dress. These neutrals are the conservative uniforms of business worldwide—universal colors of the banners under which deals are made and positions decided. These are the colors you wear when you go before the Securities and Exchange Commission examiners who must decide if your company may trade on the Big Board. Surely you won't present yourself in a white suit and floral blouse and color earrings—not when the stakes are high.

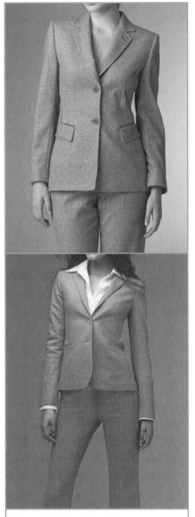

Tweed Suit by Tahari
Pinstripe Suit by Theory

7 Color at Work

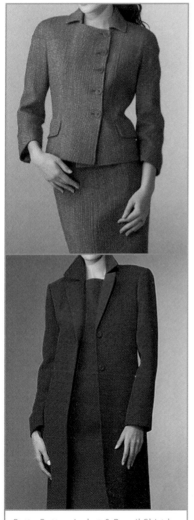

Betty Button Jacket & Pencil Skirt by Philippe Adec
Double-Faced Coat & Dress by Tahari

In summary, dark colors convey the message of authority, power, and confidence. Therefore, they should be used for the more formal business situations or when you need to exert power and authority. Medium colors and contrast are better used for staff meetings and days when a more casual or friendly atmosphere is desired.

Neutrals form the foundation of your wardrobe, especially in suits. Neutrals can be worn with all other colors, are conservative, and are those you are least likely to tire of. They have the least cultural and psychological effect and are therefore safe.

Bright colors should be used in accents to complement a bold look. They should be used in small amounts in ties, scarves, blouses, pocket squares.

Contrasting colors should be used for definition. The more contrast, the more powerful the look.

In the fashion, beauty, and advertising industries, these rules are less strict. Fashion colors and styles are acceptable and preferred in some companies as a statement of the company positioning in the fashion world. However, the neutrals still project a more formal and serious tone and will provide the most mileage as wardrobe basics.

A Woman's Guide to Success:
Perfecting Your Professional Image

No one quite understands why these rules work the way they do. There is little historical evidence that navy and gray have been the immortal shades of commerce for men and black for women. The ancient Greeks and Romans wore light colors exclusively until they discovered certain dyes, taken from sea snails, that gave them "royal" purples. The purple was rare and therefore reserved for the ruling class. It can be argued and debated that this is the real origin of today's obsession with blues and grays. It is really academic. What counts is that, for whatever reason, we are expected to do business in serious colors.

Just as these dark neutrals are a necessary and important part of your business corporate wardrobe, there is another color rule that you should know about. It has to do with raincoats, and it's just the opposite of the standard suit colorations. Beige or tan are, for reasons that may not be tangible, considered more credible and professional. They project a more solid, classic look than black, navy, or brown especially for men. Some fashion designers believe that beige and tan outerwear is preferred because it does not clash with the navy and gray worn underneath. In England, where this rules seems etched in marble, the idea is that one doesn't reveal oneself or one's true status on the street.

It is also important to note, as we shall see in the following section, that because of the elements in our skin tone, hair, and eye colors, various shades of warm beige and gray-beige are complementary to everyone's coloring.

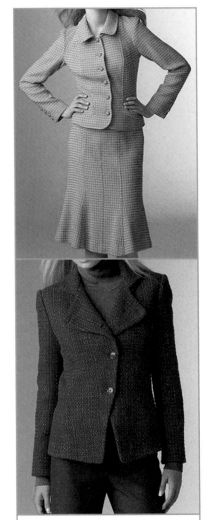

Gingham Suit by Tracy Reese
Cross-Stitch Jacket & Pants by Ellen Tracy

7 Color at Work

Does all of this seem either antiquated or confusing? Well maybe so. What isn't antique is that bucking convention with clothing—be it via color or cut—makes getting to the top and/or staying there just that much harder. Learning and playing by the rules can be easy. They are not so rigid that you do not have personal freedom and choices. They are merely guidelines that will give you the extra edge and guarantee you the confidence necessary for success.

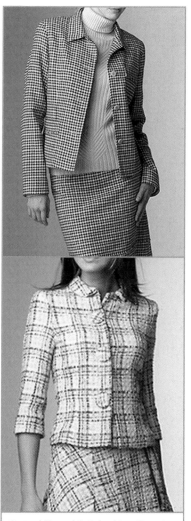

Dotted Tweed Suit by New Frontier
Plaid Suit by Tibi

UNDERTONE, DEPTH, AND BRIGHTNESS

Before we delve into specific guidelines to help select your correct wardrobe colors, it is important to discuss the basic characteristics of color and how they compare with the color of your hair, eyes, and skin tone.

One of the easiest ways to describe color is to go with what is immediately apparent: apples are red, carrots are orange, snow is white, skies are blue. All colors are derived from red, blue, and yellow. You might consider these simple descriptions "level one" of color identification—the color or the hue. But it is important to consider two other characteristics: depth and brightness.

Undertones

Below the surface: Undertones are the yellows or blues that are added to colors to make them "warm" or "cool." They are not always instantly visible. If you have ever added colors to house paint, for instance, adding a touch of yellow to blue, you get aquamarine, a more yellow-based color. The yellow- or gold-based colors are called warm colors, the more blue-based colors are called cool. For simplicity, we will consider warm and cool colors to account for the undertone.

7 Color at Work

Consider an orange-red and a blue-red. The orange-red has a yellow base, the blue-red a blue base. A great many colors are a combination of undertones with an almost equal amount of each, at least to the human eye. These are called true colors. Consider an orange-red, true red, and blue-red.

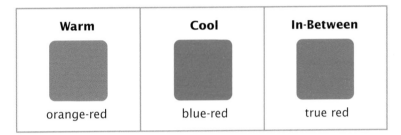

Warm	Cool	In-Between
orange-red	blue-red	true red

Depth

Light and Shade Equals Depth: The second characteristic of color is the "depth"—how dark or light a particular color may be. Consider a color from its darkest shade to its lightest—from black to white with various shades of gray in between. A deep maroon, for example, runs the spectrum all the way to pale pink; a deep rust to pale peach. The steps in between represent the level of depth. We will consider deep and light colors. Deep ranging from deep to medium and light from medium to pale. Obviously there are colors in the medium range that take a judgment call as to whether they are more light or more dark.

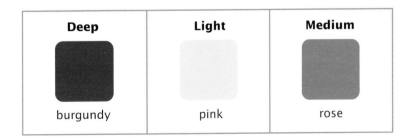

Deep	Light	Medium
burgundy	pink	rose

Brightness

Still another important characteristic is "brightness." This refers to how vivid or muted a color may be. Muted colors have been softened by adding gray to the color to lessen its intensity. Going from a brilliant fire engine red or fuchsia to a pink blush or mauve is an example of how colors are toned down, or muted. In our third color characteristics we will consider bright and muted as definition of intensity.

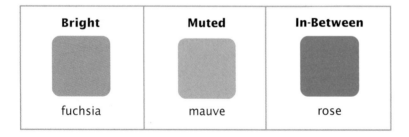

Bright	Muted	In-Between
fuchsia	mauve	rose

7 Color at Work

EXAMPLES OF COLORS AND THEIR CHARACTERISTICS

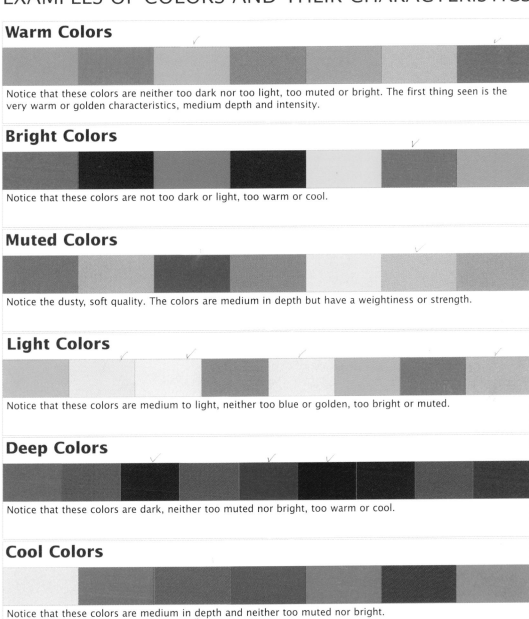

Warm Colors

Notice that these colors are neither too dark nor too light, too muted or bright. The first thing seen is the very warm or golden characteristics, medium depth and intensity.

Bright Colors

Notice that these colors are not too dark or light, too warm or cool.

Muted Colors

Notice the dusty, soft quality. The colors are medium in depth but have a weightiness or strength.

Light Colors

Notice that these colors are medium to light, neither too blue or golden, too bright or muted.

Deep Colors

Notice that these colors are dark, neither too muted nor bright, too warm or cool.

Cool Colors

Notice that these colors are medium in depth and neither too muted nor bright.

The color characteristics of deep, light, bright, muted, warm, and cool will be observed in different degrees in all colors. In most cases one will be more obvious than the other two. We therefore have the following characteristics:

A Primary — the Dominant

A Secondary

A Tertiary

The Primary or Dominant characteristic is usually the first observed, fairly easy to recognize, and a major factor in determining an accurate color analysis for your client. One will usually stand out as the primary characteristic and will therefore be designated the dominant characteristic.

The Secondary characteristic is the one that can be seen upon looking more closely. It is not usually as outstanding as the dominant characteristic. However, often the dominant characteristic and secondary are very close. You may decide to consider both equal.

Tertiary characteristics have less strength than the first two characteristics, but are present. When a dominant characteristic is clear, the secondary and tertiary may be close. The tertiary characteristic may be very subtle and therefore not necessary to identify.

7 Color at Work

PERSONAL COLORING

Your personal coloring has the same three characteristics: an undertone, depth, and level of brightness.

Your personal coloring is determined by your skin tone, hair, and the color of your eyes. The combination of these three project an overall image that is deep, light, bright, muted, warm, or cool. One of these characteristics is your primary or dominant characteristic. However, the primary and secondary may be close and too close to determine. Both can be used, or a personal preference selected. In the same way that the cut of your clothes complements your bodylines, the colors you wear do the same thing.

We can all wear all kinds of colors, but it is the undertone, depth, and/or clarity that are important. What you are after is balance and harmony so that the colors are a natural extension of you. By wearing colors that have the same or similar characteristics as your coloring, balance will result. There are some colors you wear that may not be perfectly harmonious. They can be combined with other colors to create the balance. Given the general guidelines for colors in business, it is necessary to understand how to efficiently use these combinations. The bottom line is that color must complement you physically, express your personality, be appropriate for the occasion, and current. Your personality may allow for colors to be "exaggerated." Those with stronger personalities can carry brighter and deeper shades. Those who are more conservative may want to lighten or soften their color pallettes.

A Woman's Guide to Success: Perfecting Your Professional Image

The basic elements of natural coloration focus on your skin tone. Skin tone is determined by melanin, carotin, and hemoglobin. Melanin is a dark pigment found in the skin, the retina, and human hair. It is often described as brown to orange-red in color. Carotin (sometimes spelled carotene) is an orange-yellow, reddish compound occurring as a pigment in humans and plants. It is often the color that appears on the skin's surface and can be affected by diet, drugs, etc. Hemoglobin is the oxygen-bearing protein in red blood cells and is red in coloration.

Depending on the amounts of each in our bodies, our coloring will appear to be either more warm or more cool, light or deep, bright or muted.

No one is all cool since the elements in our skin tones are predominately warm. However, to the human eye, some people appear more warm or golden than others. Some will have a distribution that makes the skin tone appear neutral. Others appear cool and pink or rosy. It is important to look at the overall coloring and determine which characteristic is most dominant. What do you see first when looking at yourself in the mirror? What characteristic do you present when your hair, skin tone, and eye color are taken as a whole.

As we age, we lose pigment in our skin, hair, and eyes. Thus, hair becomes more ash, or gray, and eye color often softens. To look younger, it helps to add some warm tones to hair color and make-up and add warmer toned clothing, especially around our faces.

By determining your most dominant color characteristic you will be able to select your best colors—those that complement you—and combine these with your neutrals and as accents to create your own personalized corporate look. They will also provide the basis for selection of colors for casual and dressy times and to identify the latest fashion colors just for you.

7 Color at Work

FOR CAUCASIAN COLORING

Deep

The deep person has rich coloring. The overall coloring projects strength that can carry deep colors. Often the hair, eyes, and skin call be described as deep. However, this does not necessarily mean dark skin. Skin may be olive, golden beige, or true beige. It will not have a delicate or translucent look. Hair will be black, brown-black, chestnut, or dark brown. It also often has a strength projected in the texture, thickness, etc. Eyes will be black, brown-black, red-brown, or deep hazel.

There can be evidence of warm and cool undertones in the deep person. They can successfully wear colors that are not too warm or too cool and are the true colors. They can wear two deep colors together in addition to the contrast of a light and dark.

Light

The light person's coloring will often be called fair. It will project evidence of some warm and/or cool. The skin tone will be ivory, pink, peach, porcelain, or light beige. It may be pale but often has a rosy or pink color to the cheek, which gives it a delicate look. Hair will range from the lightest ash or golden blonde to light brown. Eyes will be blue, blue-green, gray-green or gray-blue. They will not be brown or hazel (brown-green). Overall colors that are medium to light, not too warm or cool, will be best. Strong contrast may overpower and seem too strong for the delicate or soft look. Dark colors may be used with lighter shades and more color.

Warm

The warm person projects a total golden glow. There will be evidence of golden in the hair, eyes, and skin tone, or at least two of these. Hair will be golden blonde or brown, strawberry, chestnut, or auburn. Eye color will be hazel, green, teal, or light golden brown. They will not be blue. Warm skin tone is golden beige, ivory, or bronze, and many have freckles. The warm in the skin is quite obvious. Generally, warm coloring will be medium in depth, not too strong or too delicate.

Cool

Overall there will be a neutral look projected. This person will have cool as a direction and will be able to wear the cool colors as well as some warmer tones. The "cool" direction person has a skin tone that will appear to be a true or neutral beige. The overall look will not be as strong as the deep coloring or as gentle or soft as the light. The softness is apparent but has more strength than the delicate, gentle look of the light person. Eye color will be soft brown, gray-brown, gray-blue, with no evidence of warm. Hair color will be ash brown, salt and pepper, or gray. If there is any evidence of warm in the hair it will be very subtle. As hair grays, it loses pigment and becomes more "ash." Our eyes and skin also soften with age. As the deep person ages, she may become more cool.

Remember, no one is all cool. If cool colors are most complementary, the amount of warm is small enough that it does not need to be enhanced by even the true colors.

7 Color at Work

Bright

The bright person has a clear look derived from a strong contract between the very light skin and dark hair color and the jewel-like clarity of the eye color. The skin tone will be very light porcelain, beige, or ivory. The overall look is deeper than the light person and not as strong as the deep. Skin color will be very light, ivory, beige, or porcelain. It often has a translucent quality to it. The skin tone is often lighter than the "light" person's coloring.

Hair color will be black, brown-black, warm brown, auburn, or may be gray.

Eyes will be blue, green, blue-green, bright hazel, or violet. They will not be dark brown. Two deep colors worn together will be overpowering. Combining a deep and bright or deep and light will be more complementary.

Muted

When we refer to muted colors we are talking about toned-down or grayed colors. There is a weightiness or richness about these colors without getting too dark. These colors are often referred to as "no color" or "washed" colors and are often considered sophisticated neutrals by designers.

Muted coloring has strength without depth. It is a soft look that is not as delicate as the light coloring. Skin tone will be beige, golden, or ivory. There is often absence of color to the cheeks. The complexion creates an opaque or powdered look.

Eye color will be light warm brown or hazel. Hair will be golden or ash blonde or brown.

The color range will be medium in depth. There will be a balance with a "no-color" look. Colors used monochromatically and washed colors appear rich and elegant when worn by this person. The warm person often becomes muted when she gets older and/or grays.

7 Color at Work

FOR CAUCASIAN COLORING: SUMMARY

Warm:

General Impression: Total golden glow, medium depth, medium intensity
Hair: golden brown, chestnut, auburn, gold, red, strawberry, golden blonde
Eyes: green, hazel, turquoise, teal, not light blue or gray-blue
Skin: golden beige, ivory, bronze, may have freckles

Cool:

General Impression: Ash or cool; rosy, pink, medium to light in depth and intensity.
Hair: Ash brown, dark brown, deep blonde, dirty blonde, gray
Eyes: rose-brown, ash brown, gray-brown, gray-blue, not hazel or green
Skin: pink, rose, beige, sometimes sallow

Deep:

General Impression: May have evidence of some warm and/or some cool attributes. Strong, deep, vivid, medium to deep intensity
Hair: dark brown, chestnut, auburn, black, brown-black
Eyes: dark brown, rose-brown, deep hazel, deep green
Skin: olive, bronze, beige, may be sallow

Light:

General Impression: May have evidence of warm and/or cool undertones, soft, delicate, fair, little contrast between hair and skin tone, medium to light intensity.
Hair: most often blonde(light to medium), ash brown or light brown possible.
Eyes: blue, blue-green, aqua, not deep hazel or brown.
Skin: ivory, porcelain, pink, peach, light beige.

Bright:

General Impression: Evidence of warm and/or cool undertones, contrast between hair and light skin tone, crisp, clear, high intensity
Hair: medium to dark brown, ash or golden brown, black
Eyes: blue-green, blue, steel gray, turquoise, deep blue, bright hazel, not brown
Skin: ivory, porcelain, beige, translucent, sometimes rudy

Muted:

General Impression: Evidence of warm and/or cool undertones, medium depth, dusty, soft, low intensity
Hair: ash brown, ash blonde, deep golden blonde, golden brown.
Eyes: hazel (most common), medium to dark brown, green teal, not light or gray blue.
Skin: ivory, beige, bronze, absence of color, opaque, may have freckles

FOR AFRICAN-AMERICAN COLORING

Deep

The deep person has strong coloring. The overall coloring projects strength that can carry deep colors. Often the hair, eyes, and skin call be described as deep. Skin will be deep, warm or neutral brown, black-brown, blue-black, or a mahogany tone. Hair will be blue-black, black, or brown-black. Eyes will be black or brown-black.

There may be evidence of warm and cool undertones in the deep person. They can successfully wear warm and some cool colors and are the deeper true colors. They can wear two deep colors together in addition to the contrast of a light and dark.

Light

The light colors will be a direction for the person. They can add pastels and light colors to their primary and/or secondary palettes. This person's coloring will often be called soft and she will have a personality that supports the use of less contrast. It may project evidence of some warm and/or cool. The skin tone will be light warm brown, caramel, or a honey color. Hair will be brown-black, ash brown, brown, or soft brown or black. The hair also seems to project a softer quality than the "deep" hair and will not be as strong in coloring. Eyes will be light brown, red-brown, brown-black, black hazel, or gray-black. Overall colors that are medium to light, not too warm or cool, will be best. Dark colors may be used with lighter shades and more color.

7 Color at Work

Warm

The warm person projects a total golden glow. There will be evidence of golden in the hair, eyes, and skin tone, or at least two of these. Hair will be golden brown, auburn, dark brown, chestnut, or blonde. It will definitely show some "red" tones, often metallic looking. However, the hair may be black or brown if the skin and eyes are more golden. Eye color will be a deep warm brown, brown-black, hazel, brown, or topaz. Warm skin tone is golden brown, bronze, or mahogany. The warm in the skin is quite obvious. General, warm coloring will be medium in depth, not too strong or too delicate.

Cool

Overall there will be an "ash" or cool look projected. The cool person has a skin tone that will be deep brown or black-brown with an ash or gray tone. The overall look will not be as strong as the deep coloring. Eye color will be black, gray-brown, or brown-black with no evidence of warm. Hair color will be black, blue-black, brown-black, salt and pepper, or gray. If there is any evidence of warm in the hair, it will be very subtle. As hair grays, it loses pigment and becomes more "ash." Our eyes and skin also soften with age. As the deep person ages she may become more cool.

Remember no one is all cool. If cool colors are most comple-mentary, the amount of warm is small enough that it does not need to be enhanced by even the true colors.

Bright

The bright person has a crisp clear look. The skin tone will range from very deep to medium brown or brown-black. It will project either a warm golden tone or more neutral appearance.

Hair color will be black, brown-black, or dark brown and may be auburn or red.

Eyes will be black, brown-black, hazel, and very clear. The white of the eye looks very white since there is such a contrast with the clarity of the pupil. Two deep colors will not be as complementary as combining a deep and bright or deep and light.

Muted

When we refer to muted colors, we are talking about toned-down or grayed colors. There is a weightiness or richness about these colors without getting too dark. These colors are often referred to as "no color" or "washed" colors and are often considered sophisticated neutrals by designers.

Muted coloring has strength without depth. It is a soft look that is not delicate. Skin tone will be medium to golden or ash brown, rose-bronze, cocoa, or caramel. The complexion creates an opaque or powdered look. The golden that appears will be more reddish or copper-like instead of bronze.

7 Color at Work

Eye color will be brown, rose-brown, hazel, brown-black, or gray-brown. The white of the eye is often a soft white allowing the eye to also appear more soft. Hair will be brown, mahogany, ash brown, or soft black.

The color range will not be light or dark but medium in depth. There will be a balance with a "no-color" look. Colors used monochromatically and drab colors appear rich and elegant when worn by this person. The warm person often becomes muted when she gets older and/or grays.

A Woman's Guide to Success: Perfecting Your Professional Image

FOR AFRICAN-AMERICAN COLORING: SUMMARY

Warm:

General Impression: Total golden glow, bronze or burnished look, medium to deep intensity.
Hair: golden brown, brown black, chestnut, red, auburn, brown
Eyes: warm brown, topaz, deep brown, hazel
Skin: bronze, caramel, mahogany, golden brown, light golden brown, may have freckles

Cool:

General Impression: Ash, gray or cool tone, medium depth, medium intensity
Hair: black, ash brown, blue-black, salt and pepper, silver
Eyes: ash brown, gray-brown, black, rose-brown
Skin: rose-brown, gray-brown, cocoa, dark cool brown, soft blue-black.

Deep:

General Impression: May have evidence of warm and/or cool undertones, strong coloring, vivid, medium to deep intensity
Hair: black, blue-black, brown-black.
Eyes: black, brown-black, red-brown, brown
Skin: blue-black, deep brown, rose-brown, mahogany, bronze

Light:

General Impression: May have evidence of warm and/or cool undertones, soft, less contrast between hair and skin tone, medium in intensity.
Eyes: soft black, brown, rose-brown, hazel, gray-brown
Skin: light brown, caramel, bronze, rose-beige, deep beige, cocoa

Bright:

General Impression: Evidence of warm and/or cool undertones, contrast between hair and skin tone, bright, clear, and high intensity.
Hair: black, brown-black, ash brown, deep brown
Eyes: black, brown-black, hazel
Skin: light brown, deep beige, cocoa, clear dark brown

Muted:

General Impression: Evidence of warm and/or cool undertones, medium in depth, dusty, soft, low intensity
Hair: brown, ash brown, brown-black.
Eyes: brown-black, soft black, gray-brown, hazel, rose-brown
Skin: light brown, cocoa, rose-brown, beige, opaque, may have freckles, absence of strong pigment.

7 Color at Work

FOR ASIAN COLORING

Deep

The deep person has strong coloring. The overall coloring projects strength that can carry deep colors. Often the hair, eyes, and skin can be described as deep. However, this does not necessarily mean dark skin. Skin may be olive, bronze, or beige. It will not have a delicate or translucent look. Hair will be blue-black, black, brown-black, chestnut, or dark brown. It also often has a strength projected in the texture, thickness, etc. Eyes will be black, brown-black, or red-brown.

There can be evidence of warm and cool undertones in the deep person. They can successfully wear colors that are not too warm or too cool and are the true colors. They can wear two deep colors together in addition to the contrast of a light and dark.

Light

The light person's coloring will often be called soft and gentle. It will project evidence of some warm and/or cool. There will be little contrast between the hair and skin tone. The skin tone will be rose-beige, ivory, pink, or beige. It may be pale but often has a rosy or pink color to the cheek which gives it a soft look. Whether it is fair or a little deeper in coloring you will still see "color" in the skin. Hair will be brown-black, ash brown, brown or soft brown, or black. The hair also seems to project a softer quality than the "deep" hair and will not be as strong in coloring. Eyes will be red-brown, brown-black, black, or gray-black. Overall colors that are medium to light, not too warm or cool, will be best. Strong contrast will overpower and seem too strong for the delicate look. Dark colors may be used with lighter shades and more color.

Warm

The warm person projects a total golden glow. There will be evidence of golden in the hair, eyes, and skin tone, or at least two of these. Hair will be golden brown, auburn, dark brown, or chestnut. It will definitely show some "reddish brown" tones, often metallic looking. (The same color often appears after dye has been used or after a permanent). However, the hair may be black or brown if the skin and eyes are more golden. Eye color will be a warm brown, brown-black, hazel, brown, or topaz. Warm skin tone is golden beige, ivory, bronze, and many have freckles. The warm in the skin is quite obvious. General, warm coloring will be medium in depth, not too strong or too delicate.

Cool

Overall there will be an "ash" or cool look projected. The cool person has a skin tone that will be beige, rose-beige, taupe and will often project a blue or gray undertone. The overall look will not be as strong as the deep coloring or as gentle or soft as the light. The softness is apparent but has more strength than the delicate, gentle look of the light person. Eye color will be black, gray-brown, or rose with no evidence of warm. Hair color will be black, blue-black, brown-black, chestnut, or dark brown or gray. If there is any evidence of warm in the hair, it will be very subtle. As hair grays, it loses pigment and becomes more "ash." Our eyes and skin also soften with age. As the deep person ages she may become more cool. Skin tones rose, light-medium beige.

Remember no one is all cool. If cool colors are most complementary, the amount of warm is small enough that it does not need to be enhanced by even the true colors.

.7 Color at Work

Bright

The bright person has a crisp clear look derived from a strong contract between the skin and hair color and the jewel-like clarity of the eye color. The skin tone will be very light porcelain or ivory and delicate. It often has a translucent quality to it. The skin tone is often lighter than the "light" person's coloring

Hair color will be black, brown-black, or dark brown. There will be a strong contrast between the light skin and dark hair.

Eyes will be black, brown-black, hazel, and very clear. The white of the eye looks very white since there is such a contrast with the clarity of the pupil. This person cannot as successfully wear two deep colors together. She is better in a deep and bright or deep and light.

Muted

When we refer to muted colors we are talking about toned-down or grayed colors. There is a weightiness or richness about these colors without getting too dark. These colors are often referred to as "no color" or "washed" colors and are often considered sophisticated neutrals by designers.

Muted coloring has strength without depth. It is a soft look that is not delicate. Skin tone will be beige, rose-beige, bronze. There is often absence of color to the cheeks. The complexion creates an opaque or powdered look. This can be true with the "no-color" look or the more golden tone. The golden that appears will be more reddish or copper-like instead of bronze. It is the opposite look to the translucence of the "bright."

Eye color will be brown, rose-brown, hazel, brown-black, gray-brown. The white of the eye is often a soft white allowing the eye to also appear more soft. Hair will be brown, mahogany, ash brown, or soft black.

The color range will not be light or dark but medium in depth. There will be a balance with a "no-color" look. Colors used monochromatically and drab colors appear rich and elegant when worn by this person. The warm person often becomes muted when she gets older and/or grays.

7 Color at Work

FOR ASIAN COLORING: SUMMARY

Warm:

General Impression: Total golden glow, bronze or burnished look, medium to strong intensity.
Hair: golden brown, red, auburn, dark brown, chestnut.
Eyes: warm brown, brown-black, hazel, deep brown, topaz.
Skin: golden beige, ivory, bronze, warm beige, may have freckles.

Cool:

General Impression: Ash, rosy, gray pink, medium depth and intensity.
Hair: blue-black, black, brown-black, dark brown
Eyes: black, gray-brown, rose-brown, ash brown, soft black.
Skin: rose-beige, pink, beige, porcelain, may be sallow.

Deep:

General Impression: May have evidence of warm and/or cool undertones, strong, high contrast, vivid, medium to deep intensity.
Hair: black, brown-black, red-brown, ash brown, blue-black.
Eyes: black, brown-black, dark brown
Skin: olive, bronze, beige, may be sallow.

Light:

General Impressions: May have evidence of warm and/or cool undertones, soft, delicate, less contrast between skin and hair color, medium intensity.
Hair: brown-black, ash brown, brown, soft black.
Eyes: soft black, red-brown, brown-black, gray-black.
Skin: rose-beige, beige, ivory, pink, pale.

Bright:

General Impressions: May have evidence of warm and/or cool undertones, contrast in hair and skin tone, very light skin, dark hair, bright, translucent, clear, high intensity.
Hair: black, brown-black, dark brown.
Eyes: black, brown-black.
Skin: Ivory, porcelain, beige

Muted:

General Impressions: May have evidence of warm and/or cool undertones, medium in depth, soft, dusty, low intensity.
Hair: brown, mahogany, ash brown, soft black
Eyes: brown, rose-brown, hazel, brown-black, gray-brown
Skin: beige, rose-beige, bronze, absence of color, opaque, may have freckles.

A Woman's Guide to Success:
Perfecting Your Professional Image

MAKE-UP—THE FINISHING TOUCH

It has been proven over the years that women who wear make-up properly applied look more professional and earn more money. The key words here are properly applied and encompass things such as: what colors, what kind, and how much. The simple answers are:

Make-up colors need to complement you physically as described in the Color section based on your coloring characteristics. These colors will be harmonious and look the most natural.

How much and properly applied go hand in hand. Make-up properly applied will not be too much and will look natural. Although features may be accented for evening or special occasion with an exaggeration and emphasis on the eye or lip, for work a subtle balance is best. Remember the big "A" for appropriateness of the occasion.

Use your recommended color palettes, apply sparingly, blend and blend some more for work and accent lips and/or eyes for those special occasions.

Note: Don't forget a good skin care routine that includes cleaning, exfoliating, moisturizing when necessary, and adding a good antioxidant and sunscreen to help protect your skin.

See The Essential Guide for Hair, Make-up, and Skin Care for more information.

Stretch Sateen Pea Jacket, Tonal Stripe Shirt, Stretch 5-Pocket Pinwale Cord by Jones New York

COLOR CHECKLIST

- Color is one of the most important characteristics and choosing the right ones can make all the difference. Improvising without guidelines may be fun but you can wind up looking like a painter's palette. To focus on style and blend your colors to your special needs, review the following checklist:

- Colors, like line, scale, and fit, must complement you physically, express your personality, be appropriate for the occasion, and must be current.

- Color affects your complexion—wrinkles seem to disappear, circles under the eyes are less noticeable, five o'clock shadows disappear, and eye color is brightened. Understanding your best colors will ensure a healthy, young looking, credible, and personal look.

- Color projects different signals. Deep colors project authority and power. Medium colors and light colors are more friendly and informal. Although colors themselves send out messages, they are being worn by you. Therefore, it is necessary to understand just how dark and light your colors can be and how much contrast to use to create the mood you want without overpowering you or making you look insignificant.

- Navy and gray are the classic suit colors and combined with white and blue shirts project a solid conservative look for men. Women can add black.

- Other colors like tan, beige, brown, and green may be worn with care depending on your coloring and the occasion. Bright colors and fashion colors are fine in the fashion and art industries, in small amounts for business and are perfect for casual and dressed times.

7 Color at Work

(CONTINUED)

- Beige and tan are preferred colors for raincoats.

- All colors can be described by three characteristics: an undertone, warm or cool; a depth, deep or light; an intensity, bright or muted. By understanding colors and their characteristics it is possible to identify those that work with your coloring.

- Our skin tone and hair and eye color can also be described by the same three characteristic. Each of us projects one or more of these characteristics more strongly than the others. Wearing colors with the same or similar characteristic will create a balance and harmony.

- You can wear all colors but it is important to combine them with your own personal best.

Part 3

Universal Style

In this section we are going to examine "body language"—the silent voice that often says more about you than words. How you fill the space around you is important to your overall style. Now you'll find out what you are doing right and—heaven forbid—wrong.

There is also a complete primer of business etiquette and protocol. Though it is controversial and still very much a changing scene, we will pinpoint the essentials of etiquette in the U.S.A., including dining and travel tips and what the new working woman expects from her "New Age" male colleagues.

8 Body Language & Etiquette

FILLING THE SPACE AROUND YOU

In the beginning of this book we focused mostly on how to dress, on your immediate image. This chapter is more personal. It looks at who you are and how you occupy the space around you.

It is called body language. The American Heritage Dictionary defines this as "The bodily gestures, postures, and facial expressions by which an individual communicates, non-verbally with others." Thirty years ago, body language wasn't in most dictionaries. Today it is an industry.

If progress is what we have made, body language has become a part of it. Space communication dishes and mass media have made us aware of looks on a grand scale. When we watch the President of the United States during a televised press conference, we are aware of each subtle nuance. Did he look uncomfortable in front of the microphone? Did he tremble just a bit? Or was he projecting confidence through his body language? We often pay a lot less attention to what he has to say. Could it be that what we see is more important than what someone may be trying to say?

We will leave the verbal projection up to you. You are pretty expert at it, since no one knows your world better than you do.

A Woman's Guide to Success: Perfecting Your Professional Image

Our concentration will be on the non-verbal, the body language that sometimes says more about you than your most carefully chosen words.

It is easy to lose sight of body language in the workplace. That is because we tend to believe that our assigned duties and built-in office protocol act as a buffer between ourselves and our colleagues. Yet body language is critical to the way we conduct business. It is a vital element of total presentation and style and it may have a profound impact on the success or failure of any given situation.

The importance of body language is most obvious in the charged atmosphere of meeting someone for the first time. You enter someone's office feeling good about your outward appearance—your clothes and grooming—but within 30 seconds or less, impressions start to change. Perhaps you slouch in the chair, cross or uncross your legs, express a lack of ease with your hands, or lean on the other person's desk. These signals can overpower even the most meticulous outward appearance.

Let's examine some of the more important elements of body language:

Posture: When you slouch, either standing or seated, you generate at least five negative signals: lack of confidence, indifference, low self-esteem, tiredness, or just plain sloppiness. It isn't necessary to maintain a military bearing, but you do want

8 Body Language & Etiquette

to project alertness, confidence, and awareness to what is going on around you. Also good posture minimizes distracting gestures and lets you concentrate on the business at hand.

Eye contact: Perhaps more important than posture is good eye contact. Nothing is more unnerving than someone who refuses to look you in the eye. Maintaining good eye contact (not a penetrating stare) projects integrity, honesty, self-confidence, and a genuine interest in the other person. Wandering eyes indicate nervousness, indifference, or boredom. Good eye contact demands 95 percent of your time; anything less may be a clear signal that you are in a losing position.

Handshakes: The first physical movements in most business settings is a handshake. In meeting a man or woman, a firm handshake and good eye contact gets things off to a positive start. Be sure to reach into the other persons hand so that your "webs" between the index finger and thumbs touch. If you wear heavy rings on your right hand, make certain they don't dig into the hand of the other person. Two small points: when someone enters the room or office, rise and extend your hand in greeting. A proper greeting projects confidence, control, and honesty.

Unacceptable handshakes: The two-handed clasp, popularized by the late Lyndon Johnson (and used frequently by politicians,) is inappropriate and inconsistent in a business atmosphere. The bone crusher or "limp fish" are also not acceptable. It is especially condescending in male/female introductions. Sweaty palms are also a turn off. For a confident, take charge greeting, be the first to extend your hand.

A Woman's Guide to Success: Perfecting Your Professional Image

Too close for comfort: Respect space. Don't "cozy-up" to someone with whom you are engaged in a one-on-one conversation. This is especially critical in male/female situations where personal sensitivities can run high.   One's "personal zone" of inviolate space is generally 18 inches to three feet around them. This is safe for cocktail parties and other social and casual events. Three to five feet is the correct business distance, but six feet is considered "distant" and "aloof." These spacing guidelines apply to standard greetings, walking up to someone's desk, or coming up behind someone.

When it comes to looking over documents, papers, or other materials, it is best to make duplicate copies to avoid invasion of your colleague's "personal zone." The comfort that results, along with the signal of being prepared, adds positive points to your presentation.

Touching: Outside of visiting a good friend or the standard business handshake, the rule is: No touching! It is an invasion of space. It is also confusing. What is the purpose of touching in a business situation? Just how friendly are you anyway? And never touch a business associate of the opposite sex. It is guaranteed to generate the wrong impressions.

The avoidance of touching also extends to inanimate objects, such as decorations (especially paintings) or small show pieces on someone's desk. Unless requested to "just feel the weight of this desk set," practice a strict hands-off policy.

8 Body Language & Etiquette

Skillful Listening: Have you ever noticed that the best conversationalists are also the best listeners? Listening is a conscious art; it takes no small amount of discipline, especially when dealing with less than articulate people. Always look at the other person and notice the inflections of voice. Listen for content and allow full expression of ideas before making a reply. If you don't understand something, ask questions. When you don't agree with a point-of-view, stay calm; let the other person finish, then try to summarize what they have said, just to make sure you have received an accurate message. Ignore distractions and/or confusing, irrelevant twists of the conversation. Don't tune them out entirely—there may be a good idea hidden in the maze—but focus on the central issues.

Other points of skillful listening involve appropriate feedback. Let the speaker know you get the message. If a person is slow or halting in speech, do not give in to the temptation of completing their sentences for them. It is a clear sign of impatience and rudeness. Almost as bad is looking at your watch during a conversation or fidgeting in your seat. And unless invited to do so, don't smoke.

A Woman's Guide to Success: Perfecting Your Professional Image

READING BODY LANGUAGE

Everyday we are in contact with people, casually or professionally. We listen to what they have to say, but we are also in the position of having to put their words together with non-verbal clues to get the full message.

Below is a short course on reading the meaning behind the most commonly used body language.

Receiving Positive Signals

- Smiles, laughs, in a natural, unforced way
- Makes reference to, or shows you, objects of personal interest, such as pictures of family, awards, letters, from colleagues.
- When you sit across the desk, the other party clears away papers and other objects that come between you.
- Maintains eye contact
- When speaking to you, the other person keeps hands away from face
- Has straight posture
- Makes easy, loose gestures; is relaxed while seated or standing.
- Allows meetings to run slightly overtime
- Listens, then makes quick notes on important points you wish to get across.
- Stands and walks to the door when meeting is over.

8 Body Language & Etiquette

Receiving Negative Signals

- Little or no eye contact
- Squinting, furrows appear on the brow
- Has cool, too-quick handshake
- Places hands anywhere on the face
- Looks at the wall, desk, floor
- Clenches hands, drums desk, makes nervous or impatient movements with hands
- Has tight set mouth; little or no smile
- Rigid posture, with feet flat on the floor
- Keeps checking wrist watch
- Allow incoming calls to continually break the flow of conversation
- Acts distracted, vague, clearly preoccupied.
- Silently conveys a sense of aloofness.

Clearly body language presents a challenge. It is intimately diverse and varies with people, settings, cultures, situations; it is a life-long study. The more aware you become, the more you learn to read the signals and project those that help you make it to the top Best of all, it is fun. And as a business skill, it is downright invaluable.

MAKING IT INTO THE FRONT OFFICE

This section deals with body language and verbal signals. The setting is the reception area of a Mega Corp. Your mission is to sell yourself or your company's product to Ms. Jones, the Vice President in charge of just about anything.

By now, of course, you realize that the impression you make at Mega Corp began when you phoned for an appointment. You made all the right verbal moves, which is what got you here in the first place. And now that you are in, you have got to keep the image high.

Time spent in the reception area is important. When you enter, introduce yourself pleasantly to the receptionist. Give your name, title, affiliation, and name of the person you are there to see, along with the time of the appointment. Your business card is an added bonus. Present it upon arrival. Arrive early—five or ten minutes ahead—and acknowledge that you are a few minutes ahead of time. Sure you can wait, you have got a bit of reading to do.

If you are wearing a coat, ask the receptionist where to stow it. You want your hands free for the upcoming introductions. In most cases, the receptionist will hang up your coat. This may seem terribly obvious and not worth worrying about, but this little gesture is both functional and subtle. It sends the signal that you are accustomed to being in places where your coat has been taken care of. In a very quiet way, it says you have been around in some of the better places. View your time in the reception area as a mini-rehearsal for your

8 Body Language & Etiquette

visit with Ms. Big. Set your mood and tone. Scrub out any indications of boredom or anxiety; start pumping up the enthusiasm and self confidence. Chat to the receptionist about nothing much in general. Be congenial and relaxed; make certain that all your systems are "go."

If the receptionist offers you a soft drink or coffee, decline. Thanks but no thanks. You don't want a cup of coffee in your hand when Ms. Jones.—or Ms Jones' assistant—arrives to usher you into the inner sanctions.

Once your meeting begins, it is fine to accept the coffee or whatever else may be offered. Fine, that is, if others are going to join you. If Ms. Jones is also taking up time with a cup of coffee, so be it. But don't go solo. You want to make every second count, and it is easy to let a lot of time slip by while deciding if you want milk, cream, sugar, Nutrasweet, etc. Taking it black is better, but time is still slipping away.

> *"To do exactly as your neighbors do is the only sensible rule."*
>
> ~ Emily Post

Introductions are always advisable in a business setting. Unless you are very familiar with the person you are meeting, it is a good idea to introduce yourself and spell out your position. I never assume that someone will remember my name. I may be overly sensitive to this point, but I have difficulty remembering names. Faces and events and what someone wore is different; I rarely forget. But I am not fully at ease until I know the names of all of the players and make sure they know who I am.

A Woman's Guide to Success: Perfecting Your Professional Image

It is certainly the place of Ms. Jones to be prepared, stand, extend her hand in greeting, and welcome you by name. If not, it is up to you. If you have come with your colleagues, introduce the "lesser" to the "mightier." Between men and women of equal age and status, protocol allows whatever is most comfortable. However, I feel it is appropriate to follow corporate etiquette and introduce by rank regardless of sex. Once the introductions are out of the way, mention the approximate length of your visit, "I believe we can present our product (service) to you in about ten minutes..." Having said that, the scene is completely set.

You are now going to do a lot of talking—selling really—and body quirks should not get in the way.

Sit with correct posture, relaxed and comfortable, but with a kind of forward lean towards the business you are doing. If possible, avoid low, soft-cushioned sofas or chairs, especially if Ms. Jones is propped comfortably behind the desk in a high straight-back chair. You want to feel "on a level" eye-to-eye so you can play on the same turf. Ideally, you want to be directly across the desk so that eye contact can be maintained.

Some people feel this "on a level" approach isn't terribly critical. After all, they say, they have gotten this far and no silly chair or seating arrangement is going to keep them from closing the deal. Well, maybe not. But why risk it, short of there being no other alternative? The next time you watch a television talk show, notice how the host is invariably seated in a higher position than the guest. The reason is that the host, the star, is projecting status to the viewing audience. If it didn't work, it wouldn't be practiced by so many talk show hosts, who, it must be said, are playing for ratings and millions of dollars.

Back to Ms. Jones

Use the dynamics of business "power seating" to your advantage. "Power seating" is corporate jargon for strategic placement in a room. For example, at a rectangular conference table with the head position representing the "authority figure," persons seated in positions (chairs) three, five, seven are in the best position to achieve eye contact with the leader.

Because of this dynamic, those seated in the odd-numbered chairs will gain the most attention from the "authority figure" and, as a result, they will be able to dominate the scene.

If you are in a meeting with a group and there are certain members you would rather avoid, don't seat yourself directly across from them. Choose a seat on the same side of the table, with one or two friendly faces between you. It is just enough of a barrier to avoid possible confrontation.

> *"Ideal conversation must be an exchange of thought, and not, as many of those who worry most about their shortcomings believe, an eloquent exhibition of wit or oratory"*
>
> ~ Emily Post

So Long, Ms. Jones, and Other Exits

When your business is done, make a point of saying so. Pack up your briefcase and let Ms. Jones know just how much you appreciate her time and attention. If assistants are in the room, thank them also.

If you have made a good impression, Ms. Jones will let you know when she stands to shake your hand and walks you to the door. If she does neither of these things, her body language is sending a troublesome signal.

Say goodbye to the assistants. Smile. Tell them how much you enjoyed meeting them, that you hope to see them again in the near future. While you are at it, check their body language for small telltale signs.

You may feel perfectly at home in Ms. Jone's office; perhaps there are other indications that you should stick around a little longer to chat idly. Don't even think about it! Leave them wanting more.

Don't ignore the receptionist on the way out—and don't forget your coat. Pass out thanks and smiles. You want only good impressions to flow in your wake.

Follow up: Always send a follow-up thank you letter summarizing your meeting, thanking Ms. Jones for her time, and specifically outlining your next step or your expectations. This guarantees a written record for you from a business standpoint and is proper etiquette.

> *"The good guest is almost invisible, enjoying him or herself, communing with fellow guests, and, most of all, enjoying the generous hospitality of the hosts"*
>
> ~ Emily Post

8 Body Language & Etiquette

We have discussed body language and the importance of non-verbal communication in business. An extension of body language and total presentation skills includes etiquette. There are volumes that have been written on etiquette and for a reason. Proper etiquette says volumes about you. Rules of etiquette in general have changed over the years with our changing, more casual lifestyles. In the corporate environment there are changes as a result of the more powerful positions women are now playing, that often result in some confusion. Here is a list of basic business etiquette to assure that you are "doing it right."

Helping with a coat or jacket: Women help men and vice versa. It's really a matter of who needs the assistance at any given moment.

Opening and closing doors: If a man and women arrive simultaneously at the door, the general rule is that the person with the least baggage gets the door. If the man knows the woman well enough to allow his traditional gentlemanly instincts to take over, it is okay for him to play doorman. She probably won't be offended.

Business dining: This one is simple. The one who does the inviting pays. There is no reason to deviate from the rule.

Introductions: Higher positions are introduced to lower. However, there are cases where a customer would be more important than anyone in your organization at introduction time. Use your judgment to determine who is most important.

Touching: Aside from a sincere, firm handshake, touching is definitely out. Eye contact is important, but men need to make that contact purely objective no matter how attractive your female colleague may be.

Opening and closing car doors: If the parties arrive together and it is convenient, men may get the door for a woman with little risk of offense. However, today's woman has no reason to expect a man to open and close car doors in a business setting. When exiting a car, most women will open their own door and won't sit there waiting for assistance.

Smoking: You should always refrain in business situations, especially with cigarettes, which carry all sorts of unpleasant connotations. This is the rule for either sex. During a break or after hours the rules change and social protocol prevails. It is always important to ask companions if they mind your smoking.

Health Talk: In business settings both men and women will assume you are healthy and fit; otherwise you wouldn't be there. If you feel out of sorts, do everything possible to cover up. If someone else is complaining, don't let it be an invitation to do the same. Anyone who insists on talking about his or her health at a business session is out of line.

8 Body Language & Etiquette

Discussions of family or other loved ones: It is okay to ask or answer a few questions such as, "how is your family?" Anything more should be confined to social situations.

Criticizing: Many men still feel shy about criticizing women and taking criticism from women. Unfortunately this is a self-defeating attitude. If you see flaws in the reasoning or plans of a colleague of the opposite sex, you owe it to him or her, and yourself, to point it out. Ideas shouldn't be subject to sexual differences.

Personal compliments: Believe it or not it is in good taste to offer a well deserved compliment on a man's or woman's appearance or on the way they handle a business matter. Be very judicious about the former (better know the person well) and open about the latter.

> *"A little praise is not only merest justice but is beyond the purse of no one"*
>
> ~ Emily Post

BODY LANGUAGE AND ETIQUETTE CHECKLIST

- Body language—it is universal! Everyone speaks it.

- Speaking is one thing, but understanding body language is a silent social science. People with any degree of awareness work at learning it because of its impact on our style, our own silent language that tells more about us than words.

- The checklist is a primer for this science. By no means is it encyclopedic—it is a start. A road map to help you understand others and yourself, too.

- Body language is a non-verbal projection of personality and mood. Depending on signals sent, its impact may be positive or negative.

- The language creates "space" around its user. This space extends up to three feet around a person. Violating that space with unnecessary intrusions, no matter how well intentioned, sends bad signals about you.

- Touching in a business setting is generally limited to a handshake. Make it a firm handshake. Keep those palms dry.

- Retain good posture when seated, but maintain relatively easy feeling about yourself.

- Eye contact is critical. It says you listen well and can hold attention when it is your turn to speak. Loss of contact during an interview is bad news. Don't stare down the person across the desk, but maintain eye contact 95 percent of the time.

8 Body Language & Etiquette

- No matter how great you look, it is important to reinforce that look with the right body language and etiquette. Together, personal appearance, body language, and proper etiquette are the essence of your personal style.

- If you are a congressman from Washington you can be forgiven one of those "LBJ two-fisted handshakes." Otherwise, the two-handed clasp is out of bounds in business. It is also offensive to many women.

- Before meeting a potential client or employer, practice body language of alert relaxation.

- If you know a business associate well, an exchange of names isn't needed. But when meeting with someone new, make sure you introduce yourself and give your company affiliation.

- There are "power seats" around a rectangular table. The head of the table is the "authority figure" who makes the action happen. To be in a position to best gain the authority figure's attention, sit in seats three, five, or seven. These strategically located positions make it easy to maintain eye contact with the person at the head of the table.

- To avoid confrontations in a similar setting, it is a good idea to sit on the same side of the table as the person you hope to avoid direct eye contact with.

- Don't take body language for granted. It speaks even when we're unaware of it. Work to make the voice a positive one.

9 Dining for Dollars

BREAKING BREAD BUSINESS STYLE

"Most of the deals cutting this country are locked-up between 7:00 a.m. and noon," says New York-based management consultant Tom Pettibone. "The next most critical time is between 5:00 p.m. and 9 p.m. That's when a lot of business people get together with possible clients at dinner."

Pettibone suggests that breaking bread has become a standard ritual in doing business, so much so that the social aspects of breakfast, lunch, and dinner are merely a cover for the real purpose of these repasts—making money!

"I have to be as sharp in a restaurant as I would be facing a board of directors. Maybe even sharper," he says, "at least in a conference room I don't have to worry about spilling my soup."

Pettibone is part of the upswing in the importance of breaking bread business-style. Even with the new tax laws in place that severely limit what the Internal Revenue Service calls "the three-martini business lunch," dining for dollars continues unabated. One reason may be that professionals want an insight on the "whole person" they are doing business with, and the semi-social ambience of the business meal goes a long way in revealing one's ability to carry off a triple-A job of image maintenance. Alternatively, with schedules jam packed, the extra hours added for business meals are often necessary and a welcome change of venue.

A Woman's Guide to Success:
Perfecting Your Professional Image

It is not enough these days to look great and have professional credentials. You need social skills, too. The test often takes place over a white linen tablecloth in an executive bistro.

Peggy Wheden, co-author (with John Kidner) of *Dining in the Great Embassies*, says the emphasis on executive social grace grew out of the standard practices of international trade and diplomacy.

"For generations, foreign policy has been made—or sounded out—at embassy dinners," says Whedon, who is the former producer of NBC's "This Week With David Brinkley." "People wonder why these are such elaborate affairs. The answer is that it's part of the cost of doing business on an international scale."

Whether it is foreign or domestic business you are doing, breaking bread for dollars is an art no executive can do without. It is an indispensable facet of your total image, which is why we are including it here.

9 Dining for Dollars

DUELING ALARM CLOCKS: THE EXECUTIVE BREAKFAST

Few challenges are more awesome than a pre-dawn breakfast meeting called by the boss. It may be designed to test your endurance, to catch a glimpse of you at a time when you might be most vulnerable to an inadvertent slip-up. Perhaps not. Naturally, there is business at hand; we are not implying that a pre-dawn curtain call is a sadistic game in the corporation's 24-hour-a-day life cycle. On the contrary, it is a way to add valuable hours to any project. And it works. Show us an executive who is up before dawn and, 9 out of 10 times, we will show you a success.

TRAINING FOR DUAL ALARM CLOCKS

The boss has called a breakfast meeting for 6:30 a.m., half an hour before you normally open your eyes. He or she wants a tactical plan for a meeting later in the day with the owners of ABC Corporation, which your company is hoping to purchase. Obviously, you will need to be in high gear long before the orange juice is served. How do you prepare?

The first step begins the night before the meeting. Get all the necessary paperwork done. You don't want to be dotting the "i's" and crossing the "t's" by dawn's early light. Besides, you will need those early pre-meeting hours to get your heart pumping.

A Woman's Guide to Success: Perfecting Your Professional Image

It helps to place your papers and reports in well-marked folders. Go over each before turning in. If there are any last minute items that need attention, now is the time to handle them.

Don't worry about the sleep you are going to miss. Unless you are one of those people who needs a full eight hours, why try to force your natural cycle? Forcing it leads to anxiety, a lot of tossing and turning, and a whipped countenance in the morning. Most people are fit enough to handle a night of minimal sleep (or none at all) and still be sufficiently alert in the morning to get through a day at the office.

Lay out your complete wardrobe the night before. Fumbling in the dark closet isn't a lot of fun, and there is always the risk of selecting the wrong item. There has been many a person who went out with two different color socks or shoes. Although it may go unnoticed by others, it can certainly add unneeded stress to your morning.

Be out of bed with time to spare. You are going to need it. You will be getting into high gear very quickly, and your motor may be a little balky when you wake up. You know in advance that the boss will be pumping adrenalin at a rate of 12 pints a second and you will want to keep pace.

If you need a fresh cup of coffee to start the day, have it *before* you hit the road. You don't want to wait until the actual breakfast for the first slug of caffeine. For all you know, some health-conscious colleague—probably the boss—will have a pallid decaffeinated brew on hand. If you are really groggy, try a Coke or Pepsi instead of coffee. Soft drinks generally have more caffeine in them.

9 Dining for Dollars

Turn on the TV or radio to catch the news. It is a good idea to check on what has been happening in that darkened world outside your window. If the morning paper has been delivered, read the front page and business section. There may be an item of interest that will give you an extra edge at the meeting. If so, great! If not, you have got your mind working. It is a proven form of cerebral sit-ups.

Do a light physical workout before you hit the shower. No matter how fuzzy you may feel, a workout will push you through the fog. Don't overdo it. You would be surprised how many fitness oriented executives go too far and nod out during the meeting. No matter how fit you are, the combination of an early hour and physical exertion poses this threat.

Eat something light before you leave home or on the way to work. It isn't a great idea to show up ravenous. Besides, the fare typically served at these bouts of "dueling" alarm clocks isn't what you would want to order for yourself. So get the energy food before you arrive.

Once on the scene, be especially cautious of messy items like jelly donuts or sunny-side up eggs. **Play it safe, eat only those items that are easy to handle.**

THE BUSINESS LUNCH

Despite the popularity of the lunchtime fitness workout, the ritual of "doing lunch" for dollars remains a standard practice.

Thankfully, the business lunch is less demanding than "dueling" alarm clocks. Most of the time, it is an enjoyable event, though its context keeps it from being entirely relaxing. In some circles (publishing and advertising, for example) it is an absolute imperative for successful business relationships. Once the exclusive domain of upper management, lunching for dollars is now democratically realigned so that everyone from the mailroom to the boardroom is expected to participate at one time or another. The following tips will help you make the most of it while projecting a smooth image.

Invitations: If you are the one doing the inviting, give the guest 48 hours notice. Call the restaurant well ahead of time and make the reservation in your name and the name of your company. Let them know how many will be in your party. If you expect to do some serious talking, ask for a table that is out of the way; roomy enough to accommodate paperwork, if any. If you intend to pay with a credit card, make sure the restaurant honors your particular form of plastic. Keep cash on hand, too, just in case there is a slip up.

Arrive early: Give yourself a 15-minute cushion. Check in with the maitre d'. Recheck your reservations, "Yes, it is the Smith party of four, and we need a table out of traffic." While you are waiting,

9 Dining for Dollars

If I know I am running late, when should I call the host?

You should call as soon as you know that you will be late.

check over the menu and the wine list, and let the maitre d' take an impression of your credit card ahead of time. Make sure the check is handed directly to you. Wait in the lobby to greet your guests. If there is no lobby, proceed to the table. Seat yourself facing the entrance so you can see your guests arrive. If documents are to be passed around, seat your guests so that the senior person is on your right. This insures that the most important person sees the paper first. Place the documents neatly beside you, with your briefcase stowed beneath the table.

Twelve o'clocktails: To drink or not to drink? This indeed is the question. Today many have dispensed with drinking at lunch. However, it is appropriate to ask your guests if they would like a pre-lunch drink. If no one wants alcohol, you should abstain, too. If only one guest wants a drink, it is okay to join in as long as you stick to wine or beer. No hard stuff. Suggesting a pony glass of champagne is usually a winner. Those who accept won't be viewed as heavy mid-day drinkers by those who decline. It is amazing how the little pony of champagne cuts across all barriers to nullify objections. Whatever happens, don't be the only drinker at the table, and under no circumstances should you push alcohol. You may be talking to a recovering alcoholic.

Proper form: Place the napkin in your lap as soon as you are seated. If you need to leave the table for any reason, place the napkin on the left side of your plate and replace it on your lap as soon as you return, if the waiter has not already given you a clean one. Etiquette forbids tucking the napkin under your belt, but practical concerns sometimes dictate otherwise. Elbows are off the table while eating, but it is okay to rest your forearms there between courses. When eating, bring food to your mouth—not mouth to the food.

Use utensils from the outside and work your way inward.

Is answering a cell phone appropriate during a breakfast, lunch, or dinner meeting?

Your phone should not ring and be put away during a business meeting. It should only be on and would only ring IF you ask your host in advance if it's O.K. to leave your phone on... since you are expecting an emergency call... and it better be very important.

9 Dining for Dollars

EXTRA TIPS FOR THE BUSINESS LUNCH HOST

I am on a special diet. Is it appropriate for me to mention it to the host?

You were invited to the meal because it was believed you had something to bring to the gathering... not because you were hungry. So your eating preferences are not a topic you should ever bring up. Eat what you are offered, or if off a menu, order what you want. If you are on a diet or don't like what is served, just move it around a little and eat only what you want without explanation. Then thank them for your meal.

Wait for your guest to order before making your selection

- Allow guests to read the menu in silence. If you know the restaurant, you may make a suggestion. Do not suggest anything unless you have tried it personally.

- Before getting down to business, relax your guests with small talk. No jokes please!

- Don't allow your important business conversation to be interrupted by the menu coming or the dishes being cleared away. You can arrange a series of signals through the maitre d' ahead of time.

- If you need to excuse yourself, simply say, "Excuse me, please." No need to mention why.

- No matter how bad the food or service, never make a scene. You can vocalize your gripes with the restaurant later, out of earshot.

- Watch time and keep the meeting on schedule. It is up to you to make the first sign of ending the lunch meeting to return to the office.

A Woman's Guide to Success: Perfecting Your Professional Image

THE BUSINESS DINNER

Except that the hour gives it a slightly more formal ambience, the rules of the business dinner are similar to those generally practiced at lunch. Dress, however, should be a cut or two above what you would wear earlier in the day if this is possible.

The idea is to avoid looking as if you have just switched off the office lights and hurried over to make your dinner appointment, even if that is precisely what you have done. Appropriate dress for the occasion continues to be an important part of your presentation. Bring the extras to the office and make a quick change before leaving. A dressy top or jewelry and a little extra make-up, is all it takes.

Your professional image requires that you be extra conservative in the drinking department. One drink before dinner is acceptable; the outside limit is two. Under no circumstances should you cajole others into drinking. If no one in the group is drinking, common sense and propriety demand that you join them.

If you are the host, wait until the others have ordered their meals before you do. Take a clue from your guests. If they are eating lightly, so should you. Keeping everyone waiting while you consume your multi-course meal is no way to ingratiate yourself. Grab a snack at home if you are still hungry.

> **Do I begin eating if my order arrives early or wait until everyone else gets their food?**
>
> Begin eating when the host begins eating, or when the host tells you to begin. If there is no host, begin when everyone has their food, or if the unserved say "go ahead."

9 Dining for Dollars

If my meal is served not as originally ordered (e.g. undercooked steak,) is it impolite if I sent it back to the kitchen?

In a restaurant where you ordered off a menu, it's O.K. to send it back, discretely and without comment to the other diners. Or ask your host to help you get the wait staff's attention to do so. At banquets or when you didn't order it if you can do it in a quiet fashion, do so, OR... eat what you want and leave the rest without comment. The goal is to accomplish the return to the kitchen without drawing attention of other diners and reducing their enjoyment of the gathering.

Condiments and butter that are shared require certain considerations by the host. Always pass them to your guests first. When they come your way, place a small amount on your plate. Break your dinner roll in small pieces and butter it one bite at a time. This advice may sound a bit finicky, but it is correct form.

Perhaps you want to toast one or all of your guests. Fine—but keep it under three minutes. Most psychologists will tell you that the average attention span is slightly less than 20 seconds. Toasts need to be framed with a merciful understanding of human limits.

In greeting people, it is pretty much a matter of form over substance, so there is no need to be anything but cheerful and polite. When greeting someone in your home, office, or restaurant, correct form is to rise, smile, shake hands, mention your name (if it is someone new) and make a point of mentioning your guest's name. Make introductions to the other guests. It helps to tell a tiny bit about the person you are introducing: "Jill, meet Betty. She is the designer who makes up those terrific brochures for us..." A small touch will personalize and lighten what otherwise may be a too formal scene. If you wish to keep an air of formality to the proceedings, use official titles instead of off-the-cuff descriptions of what the person does professionally.

STRANGE SOUNDING NAMES: WINE LISTS

Wine has become very popular in the U.S. It is light, it is bright. Fitness folks thinks it is less caloric than most other alcohol (that is a myth, but so what!) and it fits nicely with the image professionals hope to maintain.

However, this brings us to a challenge that almost everyone must face—knowing and understanding something about wines. Specifically, it means deciphering extensive wine lists. But how can anyone ever get to know—let alone love—even a tiny fraction of what is available?

Homework is the key. There are worse things than tasting wines and deciding which are best for your style. Of course, a real scholar goes a step beyond and figures which wines go best with different personalities. This, indeed, is considered a true mark of achievement.

Some restaurants use hard sell when they hand you the wine list. They are not terribly subtle about it, either. No one in their right mind is going to order the cheapest item on the list, particularly if there are guests, but a mid-priced wine is the safest. If you don't already know something about wines, it makes sense to do something about it. In the meantime, these simple guidelines may help.

9 Dining for Dollars

Red wines: Complement red meat, game, and pasta. Some people say that red wines go to the head faster than white varieties. With spicy seafood and pasta, red wine is often a good choice.

White wines: Dry whites are typically ordered for fish or poultry. Sweet whites are best for desserts. Whites are generally less caloric than reds.

Champagne: A no miss selection. It goes with everything. Everyone knows what it tastes like and what it feels like.

Breaking the rules: Today people mix and match wines with all sorts of food. Nowhere is it absolutely decreed that red goes with red meat or white with fish.

Ask you guests which ones they prefer. The gesture is sensible, polite, and it circumvents having to put on a show. Some people can't drink reds because they are allergic to them.

A Woman's Guide to Success: Perfecting Your Professional Image

THE "POWER TEA"

What on earth is the Power Tea?

It is one of the trendiest new trends, modeled approximately after the traditional British event, with the special American corporate touch—power—added.

The Power Tea satisfies many needs. It provides a mid-afternoon break for those who work out instead of lunching (the teas are typically held between 4 p.m. and 6 p.m.) While some provide light wine, most are non-alcoholic. The food is generally on the light side; scones, finger snacks, small tea sandwiches, fruit—the expected low calorie spread served by the health conscious.

The power part goes directly to the corporate identity of the teas. You can expect to meet your professional peers at these affairs, which may be held at someone's office, home, or in the "fern bars" of major metropolitan cities.

If you haven't already been invited to a "Power Tea," be patient; sooner or later you will be on someone's list. It is a new and refreshing way to do business.

I brought documents to show during a business lunch meeting; when do I bring them onto the table?

Follow the lead of your host. Normally business is brought up orally after the meal. Business documents should only be brought out if your host has said it would be O.K. but if you have any other option of where you could bring out the documents, think twice about asking in a public place.

9 Dining for Dollars

DINING, TRAVEL, AND MEETINGS

Helpful Hints For Dining Out

- Send or answer invitations within 48 hours
- Book reservations in advance
- Arrive early
- Give names of expected guest to the maitre d'
- Pre-select or look at the wine list
- Wait in the lobby and greet guests; if the lobby isn't big enough, proceed to the table
- Stand as guests arrive and for introductions
- Arrange seating, keeping in mind personalities and business

If you are the guest:

- Arrive no later than 10-15 minutes after planned time
- No need to bring gift, send gift home, or thank you next day
- Leave coats, briefcases, etc. in checkroom (unless briefcase is needed for meeting)
- Do not have more than one drink before dinner
- Seating: sit so host can see door
- Place napkin on your lap as soon as you are seated. If you must leave before the end for any reason, place napkin on the left side of your plate and replace on your lap as soon as you return.
- Do not put any briefcase, package, etc on the table. If work must be done, remove papers from briefcase.

- Do not put elbows on the table while eating. Between courses you may rest forearms on the table.
- Bring food to mouth, not mouth to food.

Ordering if you are the host:

- Make suggestions and/or recommendations
- Let guests order first
- Order appetizer if everyone else does so they feel comfortable
- Tell guests ahead of time if you plan to have wine and what selections you have made. You can wait to select until everyone has ordered.

Ordering if you are the guest:

- Order from the menu
- If you are the only one having an appetizer or hors d'oeuvres, you may cancel
- Use flatware according to placement
- Bread and butter—put on bread and butter plate, break rolls into small pieces and butter as needed.
- If no bread and butter plate, put on the table next to the forks, this is correct continental style
- Use correct resting position and finished position for cutlery
- Place napkin on the left side when finished. Do not fold, place neatly.
- Guest of honor should be the first to leave
- Must send thank you or call the next day

9 Dining for Dollars

I was invited to a dinner meeting. Should I offer to pay for the tip when the host is paying for the meal?

No. A guest should be quiet and allow the host to pay the bill. The only comment appropriate would be "thank you."

Tipping:

- 15 - 20% for dinner
- Wine steward (10% of wine bill)
- Maitre d' (optional, flat fee)

Helpful hints for difficult food

Soup: Scoop away from you

Pasta: Cut flat pasta; swirl string pasta.

Shrimp cocktail: Do not try cutting shrimp, use cocktail fork and take bites.

Fruit: Use knife and fork

Clams, oysters: Hold shell with hand and eat with cocktail fork, do not stack shells.

Chicken or fowl: Do not use fingers, cut or pull segment off then cut in bite size pieces

Fish with bones: Cut off tail and head, cut along backbone, fold back meat, remove whole skeleton and set aside before starting to eat.

A Woman's Guide to Success: Perfecting Your Professional Image

Professional know how and social graces are intermingled to a degree unheard of years ago when the "man in the gray flannel suit" was a hard-driving, ambitious "corporation man" who downed every martini in Bombay. Today men and women wear gray flannel, but they are more likely to work for a dozen outfits before settling into blissful entrepreneurship. They drink less and eat less; they socialize more. One of the great tests of the time involves breaking bread—and at the same time making big dollars. This checklist will help you do it in style.

DINING FOR DOLLARS CHECKLIST

- **Train for the "dueling alarm clocks"**: the executive breakfast. Prepare all paper and clothes the night before. Give yourself plenty of time to wake up. Catch the news on T.V. or on the front page, do a light workout and have your first cup of coffee. Have some light energy food before you arrive. The typical executive breakfast goes uneaten.

- **Beware of messy foods:** Jelly donuts, sunny-side up eggs. The safest thing is toast—but without those squishy plastic jelly prewraps.

- **Dress down:** The uniform for "dueling alarm clocks" is conservative. A gray or navy suit and choose a less contrasting and colorful top. This time of the morning is definitely quiet; help keep it that way.

- **Learn to live with (and love!) the executive lunch:** It is going to be a way of life for you. Remember, it is business. Also remember that good table manners help the bottom line. No hard charging and no hard sells. You will accomplish more with your excellent social skills.

9 Dining for Dollars

(CONTINUED)

- **Plan ahead:** If you are the host, give guests 48 hours notice. Book reservations in advance and make sure you get the bill. If there are documents, put the senior person on your right so that he or she can read them first. Book a table out of the flow of traffic, and tell the maitre d' to watch your signals. You don't want waiters breaking in during a business discussion.

- **Arrive early:** Check the scene, the menu, and the wine list. Wait in the lobby for your guests. If there is no lobby, proceed to the table. Stand and greet each guest, with all the appropriate introductions.

- **Allow guests to give you clues:** If they are eating light, follow suit. If they don't want alcohol, order coffee or a soft drink for yourself. Never insist on alcohol for anyone; you may be cajoling a recovering problem drinker. You might order a light wine or a pony glass of champagne if the guests say they would enjoy it. Stay away from the hard stuff.

- **Proper form is everything:** If you don't already know how to use the utensils, or if you are vague on etiquette generally, do a little research at the public library or take an etiquette course. You will be surprised how simple and convenient good table manners can be.

- **Make only judicious suggestions from the menu:** If you haven't tried it, don't knock it and don't plug it!

- **Think placid:** No matter what happens—even if soup is spilled in your lap by your server—stay cool. If you have complaints (or cleaning bills) take them up after your guests have departed.

- **Executive dinners call for a dash of elegance:** Try a change of top and jewelry. If you don't have time to run home and freshen up, do it before you leave the office. You may be in a terrible rush, but you won't look it.

- **Make up your mind to learn something about wines:** It is one of the easiest ways to impress others. If you are unsure about the selection, ask your guests what they would enjoy. You will never go wrong ordering wine by special request. If you and your guests draw a blank, go for champagne. It goes with anything.

- **Remember the "Power Tea":** If you haven't been invited yet, you surely will be. It is a light, typically non-alcoholic occasion, and the business side of things will certainly be there with the watercress and Perrier.

10 Up, Up, and Away

TRAVELING IN STYLE AND COMFORT

Pooser's Law of Success and Motion: The degree of one's success and upward mobility is directly proportional to the amount of time spent dashing through airports, hopping on and off jet planes, and checking into hotels at distant ports of call!

Let's face it. The most successful executives are constantly on the go. As a matter of fact, there are "headhunters" out there who will tell you that if you are not soaring above the clouds 50% of the time en route to do business, you're probably overdue for a job switch.

I can't vouch for the precise amount of travel time it takes to equal success nor can I make sweeping generalizations about sky-bound executives. But I can tell you about my own experiences.

I have logged more than 200,000 air miles in a single year while my business doubled in volume. Looking ahead, I see even more blue sky, which happens to coincide with a projected growth in my international business.

It would be ok if all I—or you—had to do was fly. Flying, after all, is a magical, often exciting experience, which borders on adventure while introducing us to new faces and places. But flying

A Woman's Guide to Success: Perfecting Your Professional Image

isn't enough in today's business world. It is coming back down to earth that presents us with a thousand-and-one unspeakable fortunes. There is the new security at airports; luggage; lost and found; desk clerks who seem to have lost your hotel reservations; taxi drivers who, when you tell them where you want to go, reply in any language but English that no such address exists in that town.

There are obligatory breakfasts across time zones when your body is crying out for dinner, and cities, such as Moscow, where there isn't a drop of coffee or a snack to be had after 10 o'clock. There are cities where at 3:00 in the morning, your hosts insist on sushi and the spiciest ginger on earth. Within 24 hours, you can be stuffed, starved, sleepy, hyperactive, and wondering if privacy has been outlawed!

Oh yes, the spoils of success. You can either accept them or drop out, or fly away to a commune in Oregon where business travel is strictly for squares. Indeed, this seems to be the choice these days with precious little compromise in between. It appears that the more valuable you are to your family, company, country, the more you will need to love and live with the trying side of success—travel.

10 Up, Up, and Away

TRAVELING WOMEN AND MEN

Of course, it is slightly different for women. At the risk of sounding sexist, I believe men have a slightly easier go of it. Men are typically bigger, stronger, more assertive, and better equipped to handle the rigors of the road. This isn't to say that men don't face challenges and inconveniences; they do, in large, quelling doses. At airports all over the world I have seen men fit enough to handle a lineman's spot in the National Football League reduced to pleading for relief after a week on the road. I have watched porters happily assist women while men, weary and disheveled, are neglected. Chivalry may not be dead, but poor men seem to be closer by the minute.

Such situations play havoc with the real business at hand. Travel, after all, is a means, not an end, and showing up road-weary and exhausted at a client's office is bad news no matter what the reason.

There isn't any way I know of to make travel seem like a magic carpet ride. But I do know from hard experience the ways and means to ease the more wearisome aspects of travel in our go-go, international, and domestic business community.

ENDURING THE UNBELIEVABLE

Here are some experiences I was forced to endure. As is often the case, in retrospect, they are funny—they were not at the time. Hopefully they will not be experienced again.

I arrived in my hotel after 20 hours of continuous travel. None of my flights served a meal and I was subsequently forced to endure a steady diet of flat cokes and peanuts softened with the delectable taste of chemical preservatives. After learning that the hotel restaurant was closed and that room service was no longer available, I retired to my room and enjoyed the culinary delights purchased from the hotel's vending machines. Moral of the story: Only select hotels providing twenty-four hour room service. Bring snacks of fruit or health food bars along for emergencies.

10 Up, Up, and Away

I arrived in Sydney, Australia, after 30 hours of travel at 6:00 A.M. local time. In this case, both room service and the hotel's restaurant were open; however, my room would not be ready until 1:00 P.M. In this case, I was not hungry, for the succulent boiled meat and microwaved succotash served on the flight more than satisfied my quivering taste buds. All I wanted was a hot shower and a place to get horizontal. Nodding off in the hotel lobby in fermenting clothes does not an executive image make. Moral of the story: It is worth the money to book an extra day to avoid this type of complication.

A Woman's Guide to Success:
Perfecting Your Professional Image

Stranded in the airport in Detroit as blizzard conditions continued, flights were being delayed and cancelled, and gates moved. Instead of risking a night on the airport floor, I booked a hotel room as soon as possible at the airport. You may not use it, but it is worth the "investment."

Faced with a record blizzard & connecting flight in Denver which, in all probability, I would not make, I booked rooms at both Denver & Detroit airports.

Moral of the story:
"Investing" in two rooms can save you from a sleepless night on a cold, airport floor.

10 Up, Up, and Away

The time: twenty minutes before my scheduled morning meeting. The place: New York City. The situation: a torrential downpour and no taxi stand in front of my hotel. My choices: walk ten blocks to the meeting and hope to get a cab on the way or skip the meeting and go back to bed. The last choice, although feasible, was not to my long-term benefit. Moral of the Story: The "wet" look is not in. Book a hired car or taxi the night before.

A Woman's Guide to Success:
Perfecting Your Professional Image

On a relatively short trip within the United States, I arrived at my hotel with what I thought was plenty of time to ready myself for a meeting. All that I needed was the hotel laundry service to get the wrinkles out of the clothes I had laid out. I am sure they would have done this with the utmost courtesy and efficiency except for the fact that this hotel had no laundry service. In my room, I found myself in my weakness in the middle of what seemed to be an experiment to determine how badly I could scald myself with my travel iron. Fortunately, although my clothes still looked wrinkled, I was sweating profusely from the iron's steam. This did allow my facial mask to work quite well. Moral of the story: Check ahead on a laundry service and other necessities.

10 Up, Up, and Away

HELPFUL HINTS FOR A PLEASANT JOURNEY

Below are some tips that have worked for me. With a little ingenuity and discipline, you can apply them to make life on the wing a bit more civilized no matter where you have to go in this frantic world.

- Book your airline reservations in advance—use corporate discounts—including your seat selection. Ask if meals will be served. Order any special meals ahead. Vegetarian meals are light and a nice change for long flights.

- Bring health food bars, fruit, or crackers for emergency delays.

- Allow more than one hour between flights if stopping at busy airports (Atlanta, Chicago, Washington, D.C., etc.)

- Arrive the night before for important early morning meetings.

- If possible, do not check bags. Use garment bag and briefcase.

- Limit or, better yet, avoid alcohol on long flights. Drink extra water, juice, etc. Alcohol adds to dehydration.

- Book hotel near meetings and not at airport regardless of late arrival. It is easier and safer to be on time in the morning.

- Take taxi from airport. If weather is bad, arrange for hired car at airport. This is often only $10-15 more but can save hours.

- Check hotel facilities and services ahead

- 24 hour room service (some hotels stop room service after 11:00 p.m. This is not helpful if you arrive after 11:00 and hungry.)

- Dry cleaning

- Restaurant services—if reservations are necessary

- Taxi availability for early morning

- Secretarial services

- Concierge

- Ask about room location—to assure quiet. Near elevator? Street side? Construction?

TRAVELING IN STYLE AND COMFORT CHECKLIST

- Executives today are constantly on the go. In spite of the aura of excitement when traveling to new and different places, inevitable inconveniences are thrown in our paths.

- Both men and women are subject to challenges when traveling. In some ways men have it worse—the "fair damsel" message works to get help and assistance when none is available to the disheveled gentleman. This adds to the "importance of planning ahead."

- Book airline reservations including selection of special meals ahead—bring snacks along for no meal service flights.

- Allow sufficient time for flight connections and transportation to and from airports to hotels and meetings.

- Check hotel facilities ahead including restaurant and room service hours, laundry, business services, renovation and construction on the premises.

- Consider climate, length of trip, and itinerary and pack accordingly.

Where You're Headed in Tomorrow's New Age

Gaze into your crystal ball and project your image into the shining "New Age" of the Year 2015. What do you see there? What will the world be like and how will you fit in?

If the pundits are correct, you may be adjusting to a whole new profession in the so-called "Personalized Information Age." It may even be your second or third career adjustment, with more to come. Not a terribly settling prospect, I admit, but perhaps unavoidable as time and distance shrink, populations shift, new socioeconomic demands tug at our wallets, and the relatively cozy world we took to bed last night comes up with a surprising (though not necessarily pleasing) new look at dawn's early light.

I am not suggesting that all change is disorienting or threatening. It depends on who's up and who's not, who's in or out, and how well you are able to shift gears at the right time. Chances are better than ever that in a few years you will be tougher, wiser, more sophisticated, better prepared to shape your destiny.

If the personalization age brings career adjustments, it also promises more travel, new ways of relating men and women in the geo-political sphere. In the years ahead we will be more international, probably ordering Japanese and Chinese cuisine in the native languages. And when it comes to women, be assured that today's social "revolution" won't end.

It probably never will, despite new laws and moves that redefine sexual equality. For example, more than a half century ago, the late H.L. Mencken, with typically caustic sarcasm, declared that a gentleman "is one who never strikes a woman without provocation." Past *Cosmopolitan* magazine's editor-in-chief, Helen Gurley Brown, responded with equal absurdity that a lady "no doubt is one who never supplies the provocation!" So much for progress!

But fashion—that is bound to change. Our whole system of free enterprise is based on it. Would this be America if we weren't induced to buy a new car every year, or move into a bigger home, or transform our sexual habits, or find new foods to microwave? Why should fashion be any different? If anything, those who dress us up or down will continue to put us through endless variations of what's in and/or out. Hemlines will be kicked up and down. Chic today will be klutzy tomorrow. "Moon threads"—fabrics spun in space stations—will replace wool and cotton only to be discarded next year for good old "earth wear."

What does all this mean in a world in which change is the only constant?

Perhaps the answer is in your mirror, in your reflection. You need to keep pace, of course, but who and what you are is the key to the future. Individual style doesn't fly away with frivolous fashion. It is the one constant, intangible as it may be. No matter what styles and fashions prevail at a given moment in history, the inner you makes decisions, holds to certain elements of good taste and personal presentation.

No Paris designer or Second Avenue cloth cutter is going to remake the essential you. No outrage of social maladjustment will transform your sense or fairness and balance. To summarize, you will need flexibility. You will hold fast to good taste, good manners, tolerance, understanding, a world view wide enough to accept diversity and change. You are going to be faithful to that mirror image because you know it is more than just you. It is a reflection of the future.

That is what a truly successful image is all about. It reflects today and hints at tomorrow. Like good taste in all ages, it is based on solid ground, uncompromised excellence, and perhaps the richest of all qualities: timelessness.

> "The timeless in you is aware of life's timelessness; and knows that yesterday is but today's memory and tomorrow is today's dream."
>
> ~ Kahlil Gibran

Index

Index

Index

Index

Index

Index

Become an Always In Style® Member and receive your FREE* personal color cards

SEP 15 2005

FREE*
2 PERSONAL COLOR CARDS

(Retail Value $10)

For just $19.95 per year membership includes:

· Access to 7 Profiles providing personal advice and product recommendations on your color, bodyline, style, hair, skin, fragrance and aromatherapy.

· Twice a month beauty and fashion emails to keep you abreast of the latest trends

Advice updated seasonally

Free personal color cards with coupon from "A Woman's Guide to Success: Perfecting Your Professional Image"

Go to www.alwaysinstyle.com
Log on as an "Individual Member"
Complete registration and your Personal Profiles*
order both of your personal color cards (your primary and secondary) using the following coupon code
FREE4AIS

Allow 4 weeks for delivery

* Offer may expire without notification